AN ESTONIAN FAMILY STORY

Memories
from the Attic

The Nernoffs

D1561614

BYRON NERNOFF

WESTBOW
P R E S S®
A DIVISION OF THOMAS NELSON
& ZONDERVAN

WestBow Press books may be ordered through booksellers or by contacting:

WestBow Press
A Division of Thomas Nelson & Zondervan
1663 Liberty Drive
Bloomington, IN 47403
www.westbowpress.com
1 (866) 928-1240

ISBN: 978-1-5127-9913-2 (sc)
ISBN: 978-1-5127-9912-5 (hc)
ISBN: 978-1-5127-9914-9 (e)

Library of Congress Control Number: 2017912642

Print information available on the last page.

WestBow Press rev. date: 12/18/2017

Contents

Introduction vii

Chapter 1   The Attic 1

Chapter 2   The Nernoff Family..3

Chapter 3   The Next Frontier—Long Island 6

Chapter 4   Where Is Estonia? 11

Chapter 5   How It All Started 14

Chapter 6   The House from Michigan 16

Chapter 7   The First Lady of 9 Roslyn Drive...................................20

Chapter 8   Valentine Went Home to the Lord.................................24

Chapter 9   Father and Son 26

Chapter 10 E-mail, 1900 Style 29

Chapter 11 John Nernoff Jr..33

Chapter 12 The Love Wall 36

Chapter 13 Victory at Sea...39

Chapter 14 Drydock Parties 43

Chapter 15 The Squall 47

Chapter 16 The Oatmeal Run 51

Chapter 17 The Howdy Doody Show 54

Chapter 18 The Cocoa Marsh Incident 56

Chapter 19 The Hamburger Express 58

Chapter 20 The Clothesline and the Onion Bag 61

Chapter 21 The Junior Fire Department 64

Chapter 22 Seasons 70

Chapter 23 Tragedy at Sea 77

Chapter 24 Rebuild? Are You Crazy? 81

Chapter 25 The Tranny 91

Chapter 26 The Hat 99

Chapter 27 Out of the Ashes 102

Chapter 28 Aunt Rose's Bread 106

Chapter 29 Job 109

Chapter 30 The End 110

About the Author 117

Introduction

January 3, 2010, some seven years ago, it was a very cold, cloudy Sunday afternoon with snow flurries in the air. It was the last day of the Christmas and New Year's holidays. As I was sitting up in the attic of our family home in front of the computer, I was reflecting on how I had been encouraged by many friends and family to write a book about my family—especially about my grandfather, an immigrant from Estonia to America, who brought with him the ethics, morals, courage, and faith that our family was built on. On that cold and blustery day, I decided to take action. It was the beginning of a new year, a new beginning to start writing. Since that day in 2010, I have been crafting this work of love, and I hope you enjoy reading it as much I enjoyed putting my memories into these pages.

My grandfather's life was full of victories, disappointments, and even tragedy, yet he always found the strength to press on. My hope is that in reading this book, you will be encouraged to press forward when things get tough. Through all the difficulties and hardships that you might face in your own life, I hope you find the courage, as my grandfather did, to persevere with strength, faith, and laughter.

The creation of this book has been an act of love and passion. I am writing this book not only to preserve my family history but also as a record of what life was like on Long Island in the 1940s, '50s, and '60s. Life looked infinitely different back then, and I would like to share that way of life with the generations to come.

Chapter 1

The Attic

The attic from where this journey begins is a small third-floor space with two dormers. One dormer faced the east, and the other faced the west. In the morning, we would watch the sun rise from our eastern-facing dormer, letting the excitement build with the sense of a new beginning, a new day to fill with adventure and fun, especially in summer when school was out! We loved to watch out those windows after a rainstorm, when the clouds were full of moisture and the sky was filled with an orange glow. In the evening, as the sun was setting through our western dormer window, we would settle down for the day and wait to listen to the radio. We loved to listen to such shows as *Amos 'n' Andy*, *The Jack Benny Show*, and *Lights Out*.

The attic was our sanctuary when we were growing up. We would sleep up there throughout the years, and as we grew older, it would become our room. My older brother, John (the doctor in the family), was the first to claim the attic as his own. My younger brother, David, and I always wanted to go up and listen to the radio with John, but there was never enough time. Just as we'd get settled in to listen to our favorite shows, my mother would say, "It's time for bed!" How disappointing!

I

If only we had been able to pry ourselves from our outdoor adventures earlier, maybe we could have gotten a full show in.

I remember, I think I was around nine or ten years old, when our parents took John and me with them to see the movie, *The Thing* with James Arness. In this movie, he played an alien. By today's sci-fi and special effects standards, it would be a joke. But back then, I was so scared and overwhelmed that I slept in the attic with my brother in his bed for a week! (Okay, maybe it was only a couple of nights.)

With my brother getting older and outgrowing his stay in the attic, guess who was in line for the privilege of becoming head resident—me! The attic was really meant for kids and storage because of the low ceiling height. The sloped roof of the dormers made it difficult for adults to walk around. It was great in the summer. We would sleep on a mattress on the floor with the windows of the dormers open. The summer night breeze would go from one end of the attic to the other—great for sleeping and listening to the radio. I guess as I am thinking about it, I still have to have the radio on before I can fall asleep at night. This habit comes from those wonderful radio days in the attic. For us boys, that attic was a magical space, high above the rest of the house, with great views of the neighborhood. It gave us the room for plenty of imagination and thinking. It helped shape us into the men we would later become. It helped foster our creativity and built memories that have lasted a lifetime.

Of course, this whole scene happened in the late 1940s and early 1950s, and TV was not available for us. *No TV!* When the TV era came in (there's more on this in later chapters), the attic sanctuary days were over—at least until about four years ago, when my wife, Kay, and I moved back to my childhood house. Now here I am, writing this book in the sanctuary—the attic.

The attic now has two computers, file cabinets, bookshelves, and all my childhood toys. I also have the toys I have been collecting throughout the years, such as model airplanes and car collections. I actually have over a hundred pieces displayed up here in the attic. I also used it for my office for a few years until I moved that down into the basement. It's a much more convenient space to do my work.

Chapter 2

The Nernoff Family

To set the stage of this book about my grandfather and his family, I will first describe my family. There were four of us Nernoff children: my older brother, John; me; my younger brother, David; and then last in line is my younger sister, Natalie. We all grew up to lead very different lives, but they were all built on the foundation of my grandfather's influence.

My brother John lived in Lancaster, Pennsylvania, with his wife, Akko. He was a retired pathologist when he passed away a few years ago. I am next in line and live here at the house along with my wife, Kay. My younger brother, David, lived here with Kay and me, in my father's art studio above the detached garage, which we converted into a studio apartment. David was a Vietnam veteran and just passed away last year at the age of seventy. And last but not least is my sister, Natalie, who has three grown daughters of her own. She now lives in Delaware with her husband. We did have another brother, Brian, who was born in 1941, but he went home to be with Jesus at the early age of four months. He was born with an open spine, and I guess the doctors did not have the medical advancements in those early days to help him.

Top photo: left to right John III, Natalie, Mother, David and Byron

Middle photo: Ann and John Nernoff and son Byron

Bottom Ph Lett/right: Byron, David, Uncle Alex,
Mother, Natalie, Aunt Kathriine, John III

4

Also contributing to this story is my father (the artist), who passed away in 1996 at the age of 88, and my mother, who passed away in the year 2000 at the age of 86. And last but certainly not least is my grandfather, the founder of this family and this home and the reason for this book. He passed away in 1983 at the age of 101. He was a licensed steam engineer and was always working on engines of all sorts—steam, gasoline, electrical, it didn't matter. I remember he always had greasy hands, and my mother was always yelling at Gramps to wash his hands before coming into the house.

Now my uncle Alex, who was a tailor, died at a very young age—99. What a difference between my uncle Alex and my grandfather. My uncle was a refined tailor, creating fine suits for people out in California where he lived near my Aunt Katherine. I only got to see them a couple of times in my life.

Aunt Katherine went back to Estonia to live out her life and pass on at the young age of 105!

How amazing that the combined ages of the three siblings was over three hundred years. I hope to meet them in heaven, but not until I break their age records. I wonder what they are doing now. I know they all grew up as Lutherans, but that doesn't mean that they were believers in the Lord Jesus. I hope so.

A pretty interesting side note is the Civil War in America ended in 1865, after many years of fighting between the North and the South. Some seventeen years later, in Estonia, John Nernoff Sr. (Grandpa) was born. He was born in the country, not too far from Chernobyl, in a farmhouse. Just think about that for a second. I knew this man, my grandpa, who was born and lived just seventeen years after the Civil War ended. That's pretty incredible. I think a lot about my grandfather and history and how close we are to touching the time when Abraham Lincoln was president through my grandfather.

Chapter 3

The Next Frontier— Long Island

Glen Head 1930

Both photos left to right: Grandma Natalie, Grandpa
Nernoff and Mrs. Bock at an Estonian picknick

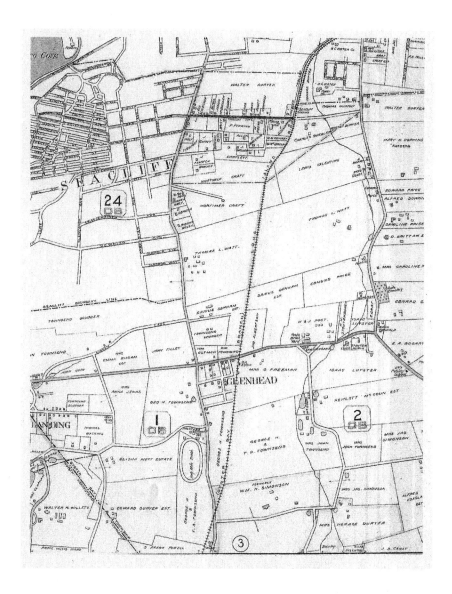

Glen Head 1900's
Courtesy of the East Hampton Library Long Island Collection &
the Huntington Historical Society joint atlas digitization project."

Long Island is a place east of New York City that was considered an undeveloped land back then. It was thought that the only thing you could do there was grow potatoes. The residents of New York City, as they grew in wealth and stature, would migrate to Westchester and up the Hudson River and to the north shore of Long Island, but not the Long Island proper itself. The deep water off northern shores of Long Island, Nassau County, in particular, made it ideal for steam boats from the city and elsewhere to land, dock or anchor. Therefore, many wealthy investors of the industrial age come to the north shore to build huge mansions on many acres of land, thus the term. :The gold coast of the United States" came from. Now the Long Island Railroad would give out free tickets in order to attract people to invest in the rest of Long Island real estate. They were hoping that those who would go out and see with their own eyes might be able to envision and develop the land. My grandfather was one of those adventurous guys who got a ticket and rode the rails. He eventually bought property in Glen Head, just a few blocks away from where he would build the home we live in today. Being a man of wisdom and intuition, he did a soil test and discovered the soil was nothing but clay with very little drainage. He later signed a new deed for a couple of lots uphill, to the west of the land of clay, and closed on the land deal in 1910 at the age of twenty-eight. The property he originally intended to buy turned out to be excavated to produce clay bricks. Years later, when the clay ran out, it was filled in with ash from the coal-fired power plant in Glenwood Landing on Hempstead Harbor.

Courage is one of those attributes that my grandfather brought with him from Estonia and one of the bases of this book. A man with no money, who had nothing as a young boy, came to America, the land of opportunity. He got married, earned a license as a steam engineer, and then bought some property, and all at the young age of twenty-eight. Pretty good, huh?

I understand that his wife, my grandmother Natalie, was sick with tuberculosis or some other type of lung disorder. That was the main reason Gramps came to Glen head, Long Island. The city at that time was using mostly coal for heat and electrical and steam energy, which created an atmosphere of smoke, dust, and soot. As you can imagine, it was conducive to all kinds of respiratory diseases.

Some nine years later, Gramps started building a home for him and Grandma Natalie. This is a very interesting house, and we will tell its story in the following chapters.

But you might be wondering where is Estonia and what is its history?

I present a brief history of Estonia in the next chapter.

Chapter 4

Where Is Estonia?

Estonia is a tiny country of about 1.3 million people located on the east side of the Baltic Sea, bordering Latvia, just to the southwest of Russia, separated by Lake Peipus. Estonia is maybe a little bigger than Connecticut and New Jersey put together. The reason I put so much emphasis on Estonia is that my whole family comes from there, great-grandparents on down, on both sides. How often do you find an entire family in America that comes from a tiny country of 1.3 million people? Not too often. Although the Nernoff family is Estonian, we do have some cousins from Finland, which is north of Estonia and across the Gulf of Finland.

Most people are proud of their ancestry and rightfully so, but growing up with my grandparents, parents, brothers, sister, aunt and uncles, cousins, and friends of the family and seeing how we all lived, I have to be double proud to be an Estonian. Estonians, like many ethnic groups of similar backgrounds, are very clannish people. I remember going to Estonian picnics, especially up in the Bronx, New York, and New Jersey.

Political Map of Europe

Estonia

Estonia started out as a northern territory on the shores of the Baltic Sea. It is even mentioned by Roman historian Tacitus (AD 55–118). Over many years of expansion to the east with the Christian crusades, Estonia became an established area of peoples but never really became an independent country. The Lutheran religion became the dominant religion as a result of Martin Luther's break from the Catholic church.

Estonia has been occupied by many countries, such as Germany, Poland, and finally, in 1920, Russia. After many years of struggles and hardship and many wars and conflicts, Estonia finally became, in its own right, an independent country on August 20, 1991 (my birthday!). What finally made this possible was the collapse and bankruptcy of the Soviet Union. Since that day to the present time, the Estonian educational and literacy rates are among the highest in the world, and it has one of the most prosperous economies in all of Europe.

There is much more to the history of Estonia, but learning about how this group of people endured such hardships and how my grandfather and many Estonians who came to this country to freedom and self-determination worked hard to become successes as Estonian Americans makes me glad to be an Estonian. I am writing this book so we will not forget our history.

Thanks, Grandpa!

Chapter 5

How It All Started

As the story goes, as per my brother David, Grandpa worked on a cargo ship in the engine room back in his younger years. There was one trip in particular though that changed the trajectory of my grandfather's life and affected the family for generations to come.

Gramps was about seventeen years old when the cargo ship docked in Montreal, Canada, around 1900. He and a fellow shipmate decided to jump ship and somehow made their way to Boston. I am told that this was where Gramps met Grandma. I can only imagine the thrill of finding another Estonian halfway around the world. They eventually worked their way down to New York City where my grandfather continued working on ships. In fact, he actually built his first boat on the deck of one of those cargo ships! I'll tell you all about that in the chapter "Victory at Sea," which tells the story of when he built his second boat, a cabin cruiser.

New York City, 1900

What was New York City like around the turn of the century? Well, from what I have seen in early photos, the process of making steel was just invented by Andrew Carnegie around 1890, and this steel was starting to stretch buildings into the sky, hence the term *high-rise*. Although the building of bridges with this steel came first and then the idea came to turn the bridges up right, so to speak, thus the high rise structure. I think the Flat Iron building was the first to use this steel as the frame of the building instead of just brick and mortar, which could only go up four or five stories. It was mostly horse and buggies, some automobiles, basically early simple gasoline-powered engines and steam-engine-driven autos. Gasoline? What's gasoline? Another industry based on refining oil so that these things called gasoline engines can run on it. It's a whole other story.

What was it like living in those days? I remember my gramps told us kids when we would complain about the use of the one bathtub in the house with seven people, that the first place he lived in in the city was called a "cold-water flat."

"Hey, Gramps, what's a cold-water flat?" we asked.

Gramps loved to tell stories and teach us lessons in life. With a gleam in his eye, he answered, "Well, it's a tiny apartment you could rent for about fifty cents a week. The bathroom was down the hallway, and you shared it with the other tenants in the building. The water supplied was only cold water—no hot water!" Gramps was a funny man, besides his many other attributes, and so he would say to us kids, "I take a bath every Saturday night whether I need it or not!"

Chapter 6

The House from Michigan

I t came on three railroad flat cars. That's right; the whole house that Grandpa Nernoff built, this house that we all grew up in, and the same house that we now live in came by railroad cars as a house kit.

As an extension of the boat kits business, Aladdin house kits came into business in 1906 and became a huge business around the country. This idea of building a house from a kit was a natural progression for Grandpa Nernoff, a boat builder turned home builder. The Aladdin kit home company, started in Bay City, Michigan, by brothers William and Otto Sovereign, stayed in business until 1981. Many people are familiar with the Sears and Roebuck Company, which still, to this day, sells house kit packages.

Grandpa ordered the Hudson model: a four-bedroom, two-story house kit, with one bath, which included one sink, one toilet, and one bathtub. Wow! Indoor plumbing at its best. It came with all the lumber, windows, flooring, doors, roofing, siding, and so on. The kit cost $1,094 and $139 for the delivery. By today's standards, it was an excellent price in 1919.

1919

1919

2017

A Fine Square House

CAN you imagine a better utilization of space than is obtained in the plan of the Hudson? The constant thought of Aladdin designers is toward giving a maximum of convenience and comfort for the lowest possible cost. It is doubtful if this result has been exceeded by any other Aladdin house. Study the location of rooms and the placing of doors and windows. Hudsons have been erected in many cities and towns about the country and you may be sure that each creates much favorable comment by friends and neighbors of the owners. The arches dividing hall, living room and dining room give an impression of size and space that is most desirable. Entrance from hall to kitchen saves the housewife many steps. Four good bed rooms, closets and bath are arranged on the second floor. Four Colonial columns support the porch roof and a beautiful glass front door throws light into the hall, in addition to the side window, and the woodwork and floors are of the beautifully grained Western fir which is subject to any treatment you like. To lovers of simplicity in home architecture the Hudson always appeals strongly.

My "Hudson" purchased last year was very warm and comfortable this winter when the thermometer was twenty degrees below zero. The lumber was first-class and I am more than satisfied with my home. Everything was found as represented and no knots to be seen. If I were to build again I would build another Aladdin. — H. M. Pierce.

See Specifications on pages 12 and 13.

First Floor Plan—
The Hudson

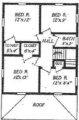

Second Floor Plan—
The Hudson

The Hudson $1,094.40

Prices, $1,152.00
Cash discount, 5%
Net price, $1,094.40

33

OUR (NERNOFF, JOHN HOUSE)

18

Before the house arrived, Gramps built the foundation to start the construction on. He assembled the plumbing for heating and water, cold *and* hot. He put in the electrical wiring and fixtures. He did all of the landscaping, and he even put in a driveway and garage. The kit arrived up at the end of Depot Place, where the railroad depot was, and the final delivery by truck was just a few hundred feet away. And so the work began, and one year later, Gramps and Grandma Nernoff got to move into their new home in Glen Head.

Chapter 7

The First Lady of 9 Roslyn Drive

Born in 1881 in Estonia, Natalie Nernoff Sr. was the first lady of our home. As I am going through the many photos of the early years here in Glen Head, I see the beautiful woman, who was troubled with sickness and heartbreak, the woman my grandfather married. Gramps would say that he came to Long Island for her. That's love! She had some kind of respiratory sickness, and the doctor thought that the clean air out here on Long Island would help her, and apparently, it did, at least for a while.

As I look at the photos of her, I notice no smiles or laughter, although picture taking in those days was sort of a serious undertaking and nobody smiled. Cameras for everyday folks were new technology then, so they didn't know how to react.

My mother was the second first lady of 9 Roslyn Drive, and there are several chapters later on in the book where I talk about her.

VALENTINE   MOTHER NERNOFF

MRS J. NERNOFF SR (DOLLY)   1928

Grandma Natalie Nernoff 1921

Living here now is Kay, first lady number 3, and I, along with Jimmy, Kay's son. I feel that sense of touching history again, knowing Grandma Natalie lived here, walking through the woods in the back, picking flowers in the garden, feeding the chickens, cooking in the kitchen, doing the wash, making the beds—and now Kay is doing the same, some ninety years later. You can almost feel her presence here. Wow! Imagine living here at the same time President Teddy Roosevelt lived here on long Island, in Sagamore Hill in Oyster Bay, just a few miles away.

Kay and I have been so blessed by being allowed to live here. Not too many people have the privilege to live in a house with so much history, especially when that history is from their own family. I think a lot about how they lived with the simple things they had—no vacuum cleaners or carpet cleaners. They had no automatic washers or dryers; instead, there were rollers. You had to ring out the clothes by hand and use the clotheslines out the back door to hang the clothes. There were no microwaves, no toaster ovens, no bottled water, and you know the rest. I remember Gramps had a little coal-burning potbelly stove in the basement to make hot water for dishes and wash and that Saturday-night bath.

I guess they felt the same way about living out on Long Island—coming from the city with those cold-water flats and now living out in God's country. It must have given them a sense of being back in the homeland countryside of Estonia.

What was it like in Glen Head in 1919 when Gramps was in the process of building this house? Well, from the photos, I can see there were not many houses around. It was mostly woods and undeveloped land. There were not too many paved roads, mostly tar and bluestone on top. I even remember when I was a boy in the 1950s and they still sprayed liquid tar on the road and then poured bluestone on top. Then, they would use a heavy-duty roller. It was all dirt roads; the only concrete road was Glen Head Road and Northern Boulevard 25A.

Gramps finished the house in 1920, and they moved in. It was Gramps; Grandma Natalie; my father, John Jr.; and his young brother, Valentine, my uncle. Gramps was thirty-six; Grandma was thirty-seven, my father was around eleven, and Uncle Valentine was six.

Remember—this book is a portrayal of life in the early part of this century and tells about the good times and bad times in our family. Tragedy stuck some four years later when the Lord decided to take Valentine home to a better life in heaven at the young age of only ten years old. In those days, funerals were held in the family house, and this was no exception.

top photo Anna Nernoff 2nd 1st lady
and bottom photo Ruth Nernoff 3rd 1st lady

Chapter 8

Valentine Went Home
to the Lord

Valentine Nernoff
1915–1925
Roslyn Dr. Glen Head, NY

Uncle Valentine, my father's brother, would have been ninety-five years old had he lived until the time I started writing about him. It is especially sad to see young children die at such a young age as ten years old. My late brother David thought Valentine died of some kind of heart problem, maybe rheumatic fever. The postcards and letters to him to "get better" from his friends and classmates indicate he had been sick for a few years.

One of the reasons I am writing this book is the documents that my mother saved on this family. It's amazing to see the letters and one-penny postcards sent to Valentine and especially the one he sent to Aunt Rose in Connecticut. On it, he wrote, "I am very sick."

The grammar school that Uncle Valentine went to, which is a few blocks down the street, is the same school that my siblings and I went to as children growing up in the 1940s, '50s, and '60s. That school is still in session today, one hundred and some odd years later.

When Valentine passed, his funeral procession was in front of the house on Roslyn Drive, after the services in the front living room. It is my understanding that funerals were held in the homes where the deceased had lived. He went on to the Brookville Cemetery, where our whole family is at rest today.

Just as a side note and my opinion, the name Valentine for a guy is pretty neat, especially coupled with the last name Nernoff. It sounds like a famous movie star of the roaring twenties or a prince in some faraway place.

I am looking forward to meeting him.

Chapter 9

Father and Son

It was just the two of them in 1924, and difficult times lay ahead. It is sad to think and write about some of those early years of the Nernoff family in Glen Head. I have many photographs of this era and all the good times this family had with relatives and friends, but it's not easy to include those times of heartbreak about which I am about to write.

Valentine Nernoff, my father's brother, about whom I wrote in the last chapter, went home to be with the Lord in 1924 at the young age of ten years old. It must have been difficult for a young family starting out in life, especially with their new home in Glen Head, getting settled in and making new friends, working hard to keep everything going, and then to have a child die with so much future ahead for him. Sad.

As time went on, things started to turn sad again as Grandmother Natalie (first lady of 9 Roslyn Drive) was becoming more ill. She was suffering from some kind of lung disorder, which was why Grandpa Nernoff had moved out to Long Island to get away from all that coal pollution in the city. Things were fine with Grandma for a while, although looking at some of the photographs of her, I see she did not smile much, telling of some unhappiness.

Having a child die at ten years old, with all of the emotion, and having a difficult time herself living with an illness, three years later, in 1927, Grandma Nernoff went home to join her son.

What a tragedy. Can you imagine anyone experiencing two deaths in the family in three years, especially with a son and now his wife gone? It is really heartbreaking, devastating. How do you go on? Grandpa was like God's Job but in 1927. I'll talk about this toward the end of the book.

Now, what about my father, Grandpa's other son, the oldest one? He lost his younger brother just three years earlier and now his mother. It is hard to understand. But somehow the two of them, with lots of family and friends around, made it through those very hard times, and now I am able to keep on writing this book with lots more to say.

My father never talked too much about his brother's and mother's passing, but looking at the photos of this family, I think time healed all wounds. As I move forward in writing about my family, I wonder how the father and son looked after themselves. Who cleaned the house? Who did the cooking? Who did the laundry? Not easy. I hope that some of the relatives stepped up to the plate and helped out. They did!

My aunt Rose, who was Grandma Nernoff sister, lived in Groton, Connecticut, and from what I can see from the many photographs of her and the family, she became a big part of their lives. She had no children of her own, so maybe that gave her a little more freedom to help out. I talk about her later on in this book and how she became like my father's surrogate mother. We, the children, became her grandchildren, so Aunt Rose was a big part of our lives as well. Our parents would take us kids with them to Groton a lot to visit her. We had great times with Aunt Rose and would always look forward to the trip. I know she had her own burdens with Uncle John, who passed away early in life. He had some kind of nerve disorder and was disabled for a long time, but that was before our time.

Like other ethnic groups, Estonians were very clannish people and with limited communication. In those days, without computers, Internet, and cell phones, people tended to live close to each other as was the case here in Glen Head. So there was plenty of support for my father and grandpa.

They made it through those difficult times, and within the next few years, my father met this very pretty Estonian lady, my mother, and they were married in 1931. What is special about their relationship was that my mother was an identical twin. Her sister was Auntie Ellen, who lived in Glen Head also. Mother was only sixteen years old when they were married. Auntie Ellen had four children, like my mother did, and we all grew up together. There is so much to write about this family and relatives that I am planning a sequel, so stay tuned.

Father and Son Sr. and Jr.

Chapter 10

E-mail, 1900 Style

"**Y**ou have to delete some of your e-mail; you are running out of space." Sound familiar? So you think we have a problem today, what about back in the 1900s. What—1900s e-mail? They didn't even in their wildest dreams think about anything close to electronic anything. Maybe an electric light bulb, or maybe a twenty-pound Bakelite phone, one per household, or maybe even a radio, if you were blessed enough to have one.

So how did people at the turn of the century communicate? How about postcards? Yep! Postcards were the e-mail of the day. One penny bought you an e-mail, or as I termed it, snail mail. So why am I writing about this subject? Well, in the previous chapter, I wrote about the life of Valentine Nernoff, and I was so impressed by the correspondence, the number of postcards that were sent to him, and the discovery of a collection of them that my mother saved. The artwork itself and the reason for sending postcards are very impressive to me. In Valentine's case, they were get-well postcards. Then there are birthdays, Christmas, New Year's, Easter, Fourth of July, Halloween, Thanksgiving, even "Happy Springtime," and the list goes on. Amazing. I have over one hundred postcards with beautiful artwork, some even in embroidery, thanks to my mother, the paper hoarder.

1 cent post cards

1 cent post cards

So, if you wanted to make an impression with someone, a girl- or boyfriend, family member, or that someone special, the artwork said it all—besides the message. I sort of like the 1900s e-mail compared to today's version. It seems more personal. A person had to make a real effort to say, "I love you," and then go to the post office and send it by mail. I have enclosed some samples in this book.

Chapter 11

John Nernoff Jr.

John Nernoff Jr.
Dad

G randpa and Grandma had their first child, my father, in 1908, and at the age of twelve, he moved with them to Glen Head, Long Island, New York. My father was born in Astoria Queens, and after moving to Glen Head, he went to grammar school at Frog College, as they called it. He then went to Roslyn High School and graduated in 1926. After that, he went to Pratt Institute and earned a degree in fine arts. As far as I know, he worked right out of college for a travel agency and painted all of their travel posters, flyers, and advertising brochures. There were no computers then.

He started working for Lester Rosen Associates in the 1930s, as a commercial artist, specializing in lettering and clouds. He designed labels for Bellaire and Oasis cigarettes, Beech-Nut baby food, Beech-Nut gum, and Old Crow whiskey, just to mention a few. Most of the ads for these products were featured in *Life* magazine, *Look*, and *Post*.

In the early 1960s, he became a sought-after airbrush artist. He was known for being responsible for the Clairol hair coloring for women ads. I think he worked into his seventies and then retired from commercial art. I have a lot of this original commercial art and many early pencil drawings he made while going to Pratt.

As my father worked as a commercial artist, he also painted oils and watercolor fine art in his spare time—still life, steamships, and landscapes. He also liked to do portraits and exact copies of the works of famous artists, such as Rembrandt. I have close to one hundred original paintings by my father of which about fifty are on display in our house today.

My father was friends with Frank Brainard, who was responsible for Operation Sail in the waters around Manhattan in 1976 to celebrate our country's two-hundredth anniversary. My father did a few shows at the Merchant Marine Academy in Sands Point in the 1960s and '70s of which Frank Brainard was curator and steamship historian.

My father painted up to the day he passed away at the age of eighty-eight. Isn't it the case there are few living famous artists; most become well known after they leave us.

As I wrote about the history of Estonia, Lutheranism was sort of the national religion, so we all went to Sunday school and church up the street on Glen Head Road to Our Savior Lutheran Church. My mother even taught Sunday school there. The bad news was my father never went with us. He was a professed atheist all of his life, along with my older brother, John—remember the doctor in the family.

Here's the good news, as per my mother. She said that Dad watched Pastor Robert Schuller of the Glass Cathedral in California every Sunday on TV for the last six months of his life here. I am hoping he made peace with the Lord during that time and we will all be together someday for eternity. Praise the Lord.

Chapter 12

The Love Wall

In 1961, the Berlin Wall was constructed to keep the German people who lived in the eastern section of Berlin, Germany, from emigrating to the western section, which was prospering in a democratic government. The streets were full of stores, businesses, restaurants, and employment. So the people in the eastern section of Berlin would cross over the border to the west, the land of promise, in the middle of the night to freedom.

Now, East Berlin was under communist rule with no real hope of freedom and self-determination. This migration was so overwhelming that the Russians ordered a wall to be built with barbed wire and then over the next few months and years a more substantial wall of concrete and brick.

The wall in Germany was built with hate, evil, and oppression, which imposed misery and sadness on its people. But this wall, which was built with this negative attitude, did not last long. Less than thirty years later, in 1988, President Reagan went to this wall and told the dictator Gorbachev, "Mr. Gorbachev, tear down this wall." And within a short time, the wall was torn down and Germany was once again reunited.

love wall 1943 Grandpa Nernoff

Now, let's talk about another wall that was built some twenty years earlier in 1943. It was built with love and caring and for the future of one man's family. It was built by Grandpa Nernoff on his property in Glen Head, Long Island, New York, and in America. This love wall is still standing almost eighty years later. Gramps was a man with a big heart and a man of integrity and hard work, and not surprisingly, his wall is a small contribution of his life of love and giving.

Love wall 2017

Chapter 13

Victory at Sea

Estonians were known for their craftsmanship and boatbuilding skills. It was at the top of the list of their occupations, which made sense because of the location of our country. Estonia is bordered on the north and west by the Baltic Sea, and being a northern country, globally close to the Arctic Circle, trees were readily available to provide lumber for this craft-boat building. Half of Estonia has coastlines, and there are many ports, so this was a natural industry for this country.

Raised in this environment, Gramps was involved in boatbuilding in Estonia by the age of nine, so with years of experience behind him, cruising the high seas in a handcrafted vessel was second nature to him.

In 1917, a few years after Gramps came to America, he built his first ship in Astoria, Queens. It was an eighteen-foot launch with a canapé top and powered by—you guessed it—steam. Not only did Gramps construct his first wooden boat by hand; he also built the steam engine that powered the boat as well. My brother David, who had the advantage of living at home more than the rest of us kids, would get the inside scoop on Gramps's life and past adventures. And as the story goes, Gramps built this first boat on a cargo ship while shipping merchandise from Panama to Montreal, Canada.

Top photo Grandpa Nernoff 1st steam boat, 1910

Next 4 photo Nernoff family and cousins, 1950's

Gramps trusted God for direction and guidance and had the faith and courage to pursue his life's ambitions; he wouldn't quit under pressure, as so many of us do when facing life's disappointments and hardships, just as we have seen so far in this story of his amazing life. At the age of thirty-four, Gramps was well on his way to becoming known as a master boat builder as well as a licensed steam engineer.

I don't know what happened to this boat. But it was surpassed by the next creation—a twenty-nine-foot cabin cruiser. According to the photos, he built this boat in Northport on Long Island. I assume it took a few years to finish. This boat was almost double the size of the first one and featured a lot of amenities. It had a toilet, which in 1940 was a big deal for a private yacht, even though it had to be pumped by a pump handle. In those days, there were no environmental rules and regulations, and guess where all the caca went? You got it, the Long Island Sound. I guess that's why the flounder fishing was so great in those good old days.

That boat had four bunks and a galley, which included a stove, a sink, and an icebox. We would eat on top of the engine cover, which Gramps made from mahogany and sat four or five people. The cabin, or the superstructure, as they called it, was made from mahogany as well. The deck was constructed of teak, which was an oily wood from South America, because it was resistant to deterioration from the salt water.

This was a fabulous boat on which Grandpa would host many outings and parties with friends and relatives. The summer weekends would be focused around the boat activities. I remember the Titaberg family with Captain Titaberg; his daughters, Helda and Elda; and his son, Henry. They would come from Teaneck, New Jersey, to get aboard and cruise the sound. I remember Uncle Henry; the adults called him Hank. My older brother, John, and I would sit on top of the cabin or the deck and with a .22 rifle would shoot at anything that came our way—bottles, cans, boxes, and so on. Great times.

I remember vaguely the discussion about what they would name my grandpa's *Queen Elizabeth*, and it turned out to be the *Trijon*, named after Gramps, John Sr.; my father, John Jr.; and my older brother, John III.

As you can see from the many photos, we kids and all the relatives were really blessed to have a grandpa who gave his life, time, and dedication to his family as he did. Grandpa was a very unselfish man and lived a very simple life. He was willing to share whatever he had. He was a truly godly man. Living with grandparents is so much of a blessing. We could share things with Grandpa that we could not with our parents. He was like a confidant and our buddy.

Mother would say, "You kids will be swimming before you're walking." Well, almost. Being on Gramps's boat and the water, we were like fish with legs. This environment and swimming were like second nature to us.

Grandma, my mother's mother, came from the Bronx one weekend to babysit David and me because the adults were going on the farthest trip to date—Groton, Connecticut, where my aunt Rose and uncle John lived. You'll read about Aunt Rose later on. I remember hanging out with Grandma in the backyard, swinging on the hammock. Hammocks were big then. Anyone who was anyone had a family hammock.

As we got older, we would join the crowd on the *Trijon* and cruise the sound.

Chapter 14

Drydock Parties

Gramps would spend many weekends on his boat, entertaining his friends, but his guests were mostly Ma and Dad, our cousins, and friends like the Meyers and Titabergs. There was a lot of fishing—flounders of course. I don't remember fishing poles. They were too expensive, so we used fishing line made from cotton string wrapped around a piece of H-shaped wood. We kids would be on board almost all the time in the summer, fishing and swimming. Even when the boat was not in the water, we would still be on the boat.

Fishing was a skill that Gramps taught us all. Take the fishing line and drape it over your index finger. Then drop the line off the side of the boat into the water with the lead weight, hook, and a piece of sandworm on the hook. When you felt it touching the bottom, wait for the little tugging and pull up quickly, but not too quickly, and you would hook yourself a flounder. We ate many a flounder dinner. My mother was an excellent cook and did magical things with those fish. Good memories.

Garves point boat yard in Glen Cove with
Nernoff children and uncle Walter.

Mother and twin sister Auntie Ellen and uncle Walter with son Wally

During the off-season, when the boat was out of the water, we would help Gramps maintain it. Mostly, we cleaned things up, like washing the windows, scraping the barnacles off the bottom of the boat, and polishing the chrome and manual trim. Sometimes we would just go down to the boat in the off-season when the weather was nice and have lunch. The boat was really an extension of Gramps. Like an artist and his painting, this boat was Gramps's masterpiece.

I remember when the *Trijon* was pulled up out of the water at summer's end down at the boatyard called Baer and Edgerton in Glen Cove. It wasn't really a boatyard or marina like you would see today; it was only a beach where all of the boats would be stored for the winter. They were moved on railroad tracks coming out of the water in the middle of the beach that went up to where the boats were stored up on dry land.

There were these cradles with adjustable planks of wood that would stick up in the air and were positioned to fit different-sized boats. This cradle was attached to railroad wheels, which would ride the rails. They would move it underwater, and you had to position your boat to line up with this boat cradle; you then tied your boat to the cradle. When everything was lined up, chucks were put in place to hold the boat and keep it from tipping over when it came out of the water. The yard crew would start the diesel motor of this big wench connected to a huge round drum around which the steel cable was wound. It was connected to the boat cradle. Then they would slowly pull the boat out of the water, and out it came. Looking at the boat in the water and then looking at it out of the water, I could see it was twice the size. As a kid, this was a big deal! Everything was bigger than life, and this whole process was no different.

As the boat was being pulled up out of the water along the rails, the crew would stop the process when the boat got to Gramps's storage spot. Then they would line up on the opposing planks, and the whole business, the boat and huge wooden planks on the bottom of the boat along with the chucks, would be led off the cradle onto these greased planks and pushed to the spot that was designated as Grandpa's. What a process, very interesting. I was always afraid the boat would tip over, but of course, it never did; it was very secure.

So, as you can see from the photos, this was a way of life for our family. There is so much more that we learned as kids about boating from Gramps. We had to know about the weather, not only from the radio, but personal observation—the clouds, wind, tide, a sense of high or low atmospheric pressure, and a general sense of weather conditions. We had to read water-depth charts and know where the underwater rocks, wrecks, sandbars, and the like were, especially at low tide.

We kids were sailors at a very young age. We learned to have respect for the water and to get used to it; it became second nature to us. Among the many hands-on life experiences we had, boating with Gramps instilled in us this basis of learning everything in life. This experience helped us in later life as adults; we had a real sense of knowing what life is all about, making the right decisions and having good judgment. Unfortunately, kids today just don't have the opportunity to have the upbringing we had. Many of life's experiences today come from TV, which in my opinion is a total waste of time in most cases, and the enjoyment of really living is missing. Too bad!

Chapter 15

The Squall

July 25, 2010, it was a hot Sunday afternoon, over ninety degrees Fahrenheit with high humidity, and we had just gotten home from church. I made myself a swiss-cheese-and-sliced-steak sandwich (left over from the other night) and put my work clothes on. I started to do projects that I had planned on doing that day. The projects were things that needed to be done at the tail end of the renovation of the family house, which we had been doing for five years. I started with sanding down the corner of the cocktail table in the living room that Harry, our new family hound (just a baby), had chewed up. It was around two thirty in the afternoon, and I had just finished sanding and staining the table when I went outside into the garage to start putting things away. I noticed that the clouds had started to get grayish. Jimmy was cleaning out my Blazer, and Mike, Billy, and Tommy Malloy were sort of hanging around—actually, Tommy was working in his yard weeding. Tommy lives across the street from me, by the way, and we grew up together.

All of a sudden, a few raindrops started to fall, and then we heard a loud sound, like a train coming down the tracks, along with a huge gust of wind, which all came upon us within a few seconds. I was still in the garage with the garage door open, so I had a panoramic view of the whole scene. The wind and the rain became really intense, and the trees started to wave back and forth. The rain became a deluge, and the wind seemed to swirl. And then it happened. The top of the telephone pole started sparking like fireworks, and the top of one of Tommy's trees, a huge maple about a hundred feet tall, started to crack. I could hear it as one huge branch snapped off and spiraled down, end over end. It bounced over the telephone wires and landed in the street, just beyond my view behind the bushes. Then another giant branch cracked off and tumbled down the same path. Two other branches did the same thing, all in about ten seconds. I couldn't believe my eyes.

Billy and Mike left in their vehicles, and Tommy came running across the street to join me in the garage. Jimmy was trying to put things away. Within five minutes, the rain subsided, and we all went to investigate. We discovered a giant pile of branches in the middle of Roslyn Drive, blocking it completely. There were no lights in the neighborhood, and everything was soaked.

Anyway, within a couple of hours, the town road crew came and cleaned up everything and the electricity was restored.

Why am I telling this in the middle of writing a book about my grandfather, who passed away eighteen years before these events? Because a similar event happened some sixty years earlier, in 1950, on Grandpa's boat. I was about seven or eight years old, and I remember spending many weekends on the boat with my family. We would cruise all over Long Island Sound. We would go across the sound from Glen Cove to Larchmont, Connecticut; Manhasset Bay; and Port Washington. Sometimes we would stay close to home and just go fishing. Many times, Grandpa would ask my mother if he could take David and me, usually on Saturday (no school), to help clean the boat. He especially needed help with the pillage, because David and I were small and could get down under the flooring to open up the little canals near the keel with a little piece of wire. He would always reward us with chocolate milk in the bottle from the store, which was far superior to the home version, made with Cocoa Marsh and milk. (See "The Cocoa Marsh Incident" later on in the book.)

Sometime that summer of 1949 or 1950, the whole family went on Grandpa's boat to Lloyd's Harbor, which is on the north shore of long Island near Huntington. It was like a lagoon, something like the lagoon in the TV series *Gilligan's Island*. We would have a great time there. We would sleep over in the boat, and I guess Grandpa, my father, and my brother would sleep on the shore in a tent not too far from the boat, maybe a few hundred yards away. The boat had a little boat that it would tow along with us, called the dingy, with oars (no outboards), which they would use to get to the beach and back.

I remember we would jump off the bow of the boat into the water feet first, but as we got older, well, then it was from the top of the cabin and headfirst. The boat was called a cabin cruiser.

I remember that Sunday, my grandfather was suggesting to my father that they should really get going home, for the weather wasn't looking good. They lifted anchor and started heading out of the Lloyd's Neck lagoon back toward Glen Cove Harbor. That trek started out going toward Bayville. Eventually, we would go to Glen Cove Harbor and then to the dock where Grandpa would drop everyone off. Then he would go to the mooring, which was in Glen Cove Harbor, tie up the boat, and row into shore in the dingy.

As we were on our way, the weather all of a sudden started whipping up, and the waves started to come over the bow of the boat. Water was coming in under the windshield, and I remember the water running horizontally along the windows on the side of the cabin. My mother ordered us kids to go into the galley and get into the bunks. My father, who was a big chicken, started panicking and even though he was an atheist at that time, starting praying to God, "Please save us! Please save us!" I remember at one point the waves were not only coming over the bow but also coming over the cabin and landing in the back of the boat where we would sit.

People in a sailboat were screaming for us to help them, as their mast was broken in half, but I heard my Grandpa yell back that we could not help, for we were in big trouble ourselves. The wind was like that of the day I described in Glen Head; it just came on all of a sudden. As we were approaching the Glen Cove area, my father asked Grandpa to just go into the harbor. Gramps said, "No, we must head into the waves and then come around." We kept going back and forth until we got in a little closer. If we had just headed straight into the harbor, we would have been broadsided by the waves and flipped over. Gramps was a great seaman, with lots of courage and faith.

It seemed like an eternity, filled with fear and trepidation, but we made it. There is one incident that still stands out in my mind so clearly, and that is when my mother came down into the galley to check on us kids. She found a can of Maxwell House opened with no lid on the floor of the galley and not one grain of coffee spilled. That can of coffee had started out on the counter in the galley's kitchen. Amazing.

Chapter 16

The Oatmeal Run

S aturday mornings today are the same as they were years ago. We, kids, like our parents, would look forward to Saturday mornings, but our Saturday mornings were special—Gramps was home.

During the week, Gramps would get up early to go to work at around five in the morning and would head off to the city. Actually, he worked in Long Island City at the National Casket Company, where he would run the company as a steam engineer. He was in charge of the operation of all the saws, drill presses, and sanding machines that all ran off a huge complex of drafts, belts, and pulleys, powered by steam engines—all to make caskets. Anyway, Gramps would get up early on Saturday still, maybe not at five in the morning, but early enough. He would make coffee, using real ground coffee—I think Maxwell House—in a coffeepot that would be perked, fry up a pound of bacon, and make toast from slices of Estonian babka and, of course, oatmeal. Boy oh boy, we would have such a great time having breakfast with Gramps. It was just David and I in the early years, as seen in the photo, and then my sister, Natalie, would join the gang when she got a little older. Of course, my parents and older brother, John, would have breakfast as well, but the real guests were David and I in our own little world with Gramps.

Gramps would tell us of this place near where he worked, this Shangri-La magical place where they made and served you oatmeal at a counter while you sat on a stool. Can you imagine this distant place, in what could have been in a foreign country, where they ate oatmeal? Anyway, David, Gramps, and I continued having our Saturday-morning get-together, and we were always asking Gramps about this Shangri-La place. And then it happened. One day, he posed the question, "You guys want to come to work with me and I will take you to that place—the Lunch Room?" Always remember that term, *the Lunch Room*.

So the big day came when we settled down in Gramps's 1951 Henry J. Today, we would be buckled up, but there were no seat belts back then so we settled in and off we went. I am sure Ma told Gramps a million times, "Make sure you watch those kids and don't let anything happen to them!"

In 1950, there was no Long Island Expressway and no Roslyn Viaduct. We drove all the way to Long Island City by taking Northern Boulevard. We knew we were getting closer because of the changes in the landscape. The grass and trees were being replaced by buildings and sidewalks. And then there it was, the building where Gramps worked, surrounded by those overhead railroad trains. Two wide-eyed kids in the big city—we were speechless!

I remember Gramps's office with his desk, machine parts all around, boilers, pipes, valves, and the hissing noise of steam licking through so many pipes. We could hear the clacking and ticking of the steam engines and all of the different components, all connected to this big shaft up near the ceiling with leather straps—lots of excitement, sights, and sounds! I especially remember a big, open-ended wrench hanging on the wall in Grandpa's office.

Then the big moment came. We followed Gramps out of the office and down the street not too far, and there it was—the Lunch Room.

As we walked in, Gramps introduced us to all of his friends and the guys he worked with. "Hey, guys, meet my grandkids!"

We sat down on these things called stools with our legs dangling, and Gramps said to this guy behind the counter wearing a paper hat, "Bring us three oatmeals please!"

Wow. We looked at the bowls of oatmeal, David and I, and we couldn't believe it. It was the same oatmeal we would have at home. We added sugar and I think cream, unlike the home version with just ordinary milk. We had a great time with Gramps, and we were so proud of him. He was our hero, and we probably talked about the big trip to the city for weeks after.

Chapter 17

The Howdy Doody Show

Nineteen fifty-one was the year that changed our lives forever. It was the year my father brought home one of those magic boxes; we could actually see people talking and walking around on the lighted glass screen. It was television. It was such a big event that my mother put the date of the photo on this page with not only the year, which she did with all of the photos in this book, but the day and month—April 10, 1951.

Just as a side note, I am able to put this book together because of my mother. She saved and categorized all of these photographs and dated every one. My mother was a saver, and she would save and reuse everything. Nothing went to waste. I will talk about the hand-me-down and reuse-everything generation later in this book.

TV—what a blessing and what a curse! As we talked about in the beginning of this book, in the chapter called "The Attic," this thing called TV ended those radio days as we knew them. We Nernoff kids had a big advantage over the other kids at school in reference to TV. We had a secret agent who told us about this new contraption years ahead of everyone else. That secret agent was Mr. Carroll. Now, Mr. Carroll was Randy and Steven's father and lived up the street on Depot Place. He was a pilot during World War II and then for TWA. He later became a radio and TV repair guy, operating his own business. He had this latest invention several years before everyone else.

Well, needless to say, the Carroll kids were our best friends. Why? Because we would go to the Carroll house most days after school and watch such shows as *The Howdy Doody Show*; *Kukla, Fran, and Ollie*; *The Lone Ranger*; and many more. Needless to say, this is why we kids ended up so stupid—the curse.

My father finally saved up enough money and bought our own family TV. It was an RCA with a big twelve-inch screen. What an event, watching TV in the comfort of our own home! The first show we saw with this new toy was the Arthur Godfrey show. There were limited hours of broadcasting, I think from around three or four in the afternoon until maybe nine or ten at night. And, of course, we would watch *The Howdy Doody Show* with Claribel and Bob Smith.

After we got our own TV, our best friends with the first neighborhood TV, the Carroll boys ... Who? What Carroll boys? Just kidding—they still are good friends.

Chapter 18

The Cocoa Marsh Incident

It was 1949, and I was seven years old and going to Glen Head Grammar School. We used to walk, as it was just a couple of blocks. That's the same school my uncle Valentine went to twenty-five years earlier. My mother used to babysit during the day to help with the finances of the house because my father was one of those starving artists and things were kind of tight.

We would get home after school in the afternoon, and since my mother was usually babysitting, we were left to our own devices until she got home. I loved chocolate milk, as I mentioned in the squall story, and I would take out the Cocoa Marsh jar, a glass, a spoon, and the milk, all displayed on the kitchen table. Now Cocoa Marsh was the name of a brand of chocolate syrup, like Hershey's Chocolate Syrup today. But there were no plastic containers then, only real glass jars with metal screw tops. Without fail, the whole thing would get messy with chocolate syrup dripping down the sides of the jar and all over the metal lid and so forth.

Anyway, after the chocolate cocktail was made and consumed, I would, as a young boy with his mind on getting outside as quickly as possible, leave everything on the kitchen table. Can you picture it? An open jar of chocolate syrup with the syrup dripping down the side, the lid full of syrup as well, just sitting there … beside it an empty glass and a dirty spoon, all sitting on a sloppy tablecloth with drops of chocolate milk all over!

Well, my mother would get home and find this mess, and I would hear it. "Byron! You have to clean up after yourself!" Whatever my mother said, it would go through one ear and right out the other. Well, Ma said, "The next time you leave the Cocoa Marsh display on the table, I am going to pour it over your head!" Needless to say, I continued this practice until one night at dinner, it happened!

Everyone was looking at my mother, who was positioned behind me, and I was puzzled as to why. And that's when I felt this wet substance dripping down my neck. It was the Cocoa Marsh syrup, as promised. Everyone at the table was in a state of shock, though there was some snickering. I guess my head must have looked like the head of a wet cat.

Ma escorted me to the upstairs bathroom and into the tub. I remember the bathwater being this shade of chocolate brown, and boy was I embarrassed. Needless to say, that was the end of the Cocoa Marsh episodes. I still like chocolate milk today, but I am very careful that I clean up after myself, for fear I might have to take a shower if I leave the mess and Kay has to clean up.

Chapter 19

The Hamburger Express

Byron, Natalie and David

Well, my mother was babysitting again, and yours truly had the privilege of doing the cooking. This time, it was lunch. Anyway, Ma asked me, "Byron, can you cook some hamburgers for your brother and sister? I have to go sit for Mrs. So-and-So?" Now we did not call them burgers then; they were hamburgers. The shortened version of *burgers* didn't really start being used until the 1960s when Burger King and McDonald's came into business.

My brother David, whom we will call the instigator; my sister, Natalie; and I had reservations at the kitchen table for lunch. As David and I were preparing the hamburger meat, Dave suggested that maybe just for fun we should add a little dog food into Natalie's hamburger meat. Now Gramps would feed Jippy, our family dog, this dog food called Kennel Ration, which came out of the can and looked like corned beef hash. So for the great chef I would become, this would be a good start toward my career. We did it. We added just a little of this hamburger helper to Natalie's gourmet lunch. We figured if Jippy didn't get sick or die from his food—and we had heard about poor, starving people around the world eating dog food—it would be okay for our sister. At the same time, we could have a few laughs together.

The hamburgers were cooked; put on the rolls, with lettuce, tomatoes, and mayo; and set on the plate. David and I yelled upstairs for Natalie to come down and eat. She did, and when lunch was over, we asked her, "How was the hamburger?"

She said, "Great, delicious." But figuring something was up for us to even ask, she asked, "Why? Why do you ask?"

"Oh nothing, just wanted to know," we said with a giggle in our voices.

"Come on … What's so funny?" she said.

"Nothing …" came the reply.

But she wouldn't give up. "What did you guys do with my hamburger?"

Just some more giggling.

"I'm going to tell Ma!"

Well, I can't remember what happened after that exactly or how Ma found out, but David got blamed for the whole thing. According to Natalie, the burger was delicious, so what can I tell you, from an up-and-coming chef?

Side note—the title of this chapter is "The Hamburger Express" for obvious reasons. It was also the name of a hamburger place down in Glen Cove, which was the big city then, where my father took us kids to have lunch. But if you sat at the counter, your order would be delivered to you by railroad—I mean by Lionel trains that had plates attached to flat cars. Your hamburger would stop right in front of you. You would take the plates off the train and eat. What fun! And I really think my father had more fun than we, for he was into toy trains big-time.

Chapter 20

The Clothesline and the Onion Bag

As we were growing up here in Glen Head, we would have different activities throughout the years, and we called them "seasons." Well, this season was peashooter season, and if you were good at it, you would be like the king of the hill. By the way, do you remember playing king of the hill? Anyway, for those who are not really familiar with what a peashooter is, they were straws, which in those days were little round tubes made out of paper and coated with wax. The normal use for them was to drink soda and egg creams. Egg creams? What's an egg cream? It is a drink made with chocolate syrup going first in the glass and then milk poured in next. It is then topped with carbonated water and stirred. Delicious.

Getting back to those straws ... We kids had another use for them: shooting spit balls through them. Spit balls were little round balls that were made out of any piece of paper and some saliva and fit down the end of the straw. Once in the breach of the straw and with the pressure of a good hard blow from one end of the straw, the little round paper ball would fly out. And if you were good at target practice, you would hit the enemy and you had your kill.

As time went on, we would get more daring with target practice and would expand our choice of prey from the playground and home to the classroom. I think we were in fourth or fifth grade. But as progress never ceases and with the advancement of technology, a new type of straw was discovered; it was made out of this new material called "plastic." What a find! It was like a bazooka compared to a .22-caliber rifle. This new advancement in weaponry was uncovered at Koch's General Store, which is a story in itself.

Wait a minute! This chapter is named "The Clothesline and the Onion Bag," what does that have to do with a peashooter? Wait. It's coming.

So like everything else, we had to have the latest in fun fighting equipment, and these new bazooka straws would have the capacity to use dried green peas as ammo. If those weren't available, we could use split peas, which my mother had in the kitchen cabinet for when she made split-pea soup. Boy oh boy, this new ammo with plastic straws would have some impact on the enemy.

But one day on one of our safaris, my friend from across the street on Depot Place, Tommy Malloy, and I discovered this huge tree up by the Long Island railroad tracks. It had, hanging all around its trunk, these little green berries. Let's see now. "Hey, Tommy! Wouldn't these little green berries make great ammo for our new plastic shooters?"

He replied, "Byron, you're right! Let's try them out!"

You see, we had been looking all over the world (Glen Head) for something better than those split peas, which were not exactly round. They would lose air pressure, which resulted in less firepower. But these little green berries, hanging from this vine around the tree, were round and fit perfectly in the barrel of the plastic bazookas. This now made Tommy and me two guys to be reckoned with. That was it. You couldn't touch us; we had the super ammo and the place of the top-secret supply.

But the enemy struck from behind the lines. It was in the form of a rash, and we couldn't figure it out. This rash started getting worse. Legs and hands started swelling up and turning red. It got so bad that the medicvac was called in, also known as Dr. Burns, the family doctor. In those days, house visits were a standard practice, not like today where you have to have a referral or you die.

The diagnosis was … ready? Poison oak. Yep, those little green berries hanging from the tree up at the railroad tracks were poison oak. Tommy and I were actually eating them, besides just shooting them, and we were covered with this rash from head to toe. My mother had some time putting calamine lotion on me. So after a few days of intensive care, we were starting to recover. I remember lying in bed, arms and legs spread out, and my mother coming in for her hospital rounds, cotton-balling me with this lotion.

Here's where the clothesline and the onion bag come in. To keep Tommy and me amused during this recovery stage, my grandfather and Mr. Malloy, Tommy's father, rigged up this clothesline with pulleys and strung it between the two houses. It went from our bathroom window to Tommy's bedroom window, which was about fifty feet or so across the street. An empty onion bag, also made from this new material called plastic, was attached to the clothesline, and Tommy and I would exchange stuff like comic books, toys, drawings, and so on to keep ourselves amused.

It was really ingenious and thoughtful of Gramps and Red Malloy to do that for us. It was real down-to-earth love.

Anyway, the war was over, and we kids recovered from our wounds, and from then on, every time I work in the garden, I wear gloves so I won't get some kind of poison ivy or something that causes a rash. I always think about those days up at the big tree near the railroad tracks.

Chapter 21

The Junior Fire Department

The fire bell started to ring, and all of the volunteers scrambled from everywhere: 9 Roslyn Drive, 11 Roslyn Drive, and 2 Depot Place. The fire was reported in at 11:34 a.m., and within minutes, the first to arrive at the scene was the pumper truck from 9 Roslyn Drive. It had the latest in firefighting equipment: the Siamese-twin water connection. Next to arrive was the hook and ladder from the fire station at 11 Roslyn Drive, and finally the chemical truck arrived from up the street at 2 Depot Place, which saved the day, for this was a difficult blaze to put out. Within minutes, the fire was under control, and all of the trucks were repacked with their gear. The firemen went over to the driveway at 9 Roslyn Drive for a Kool-Aid break.

If you hadn't realized by now, all of the volunteer firemen were between five and eight years old. In 1950, we established the first junior fire company in Glen Head.

Byron Nernoff, Chief
Tom Malloy, Deputy Chief
Dave Nernoff, Assistant to the Chief

Johnny Malloy, First Deputy
Randy and Steven Carroll, Specialists in Difficult Fires

(Steven was known as Rodan, and they had a specially designed chemical truck with the latest in sand-bucket technology.)

The fire bell was an extra bell my grandfather had from one of his boats. The Siamese-twin water connection was actually from Father's lawn equipment. He would use it to water the lawn with two hoses, and the sand came from Mr. Carroll. He was using the sand to do some concrete work at their house.

All of the trucks were converted soapbox derby racers from another era. You see, we had the freedom from technology, and we would, with the guidance of Grandpa Nernoff, use our imaginations and our hands to create our own little world. As a side note, at that time, by law, we were allowed to burn leaves in the fall on the curbs of the road, so making fires out of cardboard boxes and then putting them out was not too far from reality.

John, Byron And David Burning Leaves

As we got older, we would become more daring, which leads me to the story of the last big fire in the back woods. As we grew up in the late 1940s and '50s, we were used to fixing, building, and creating things from our dreams, and one of those was a house we built in the woods in the back of my grandfather's property, the back lot. We were allowed to be creative and explore, and one of those projects was a little playhouse called "the Hut." We built it with a potbelly stove, a real window, cedar shingles, and a loft, and of course, under the floorboards was a secret compartment where we would hide those early *Playboy* magazines. Maybe we even had the first one with Marilyn Monroe on the cover, which would now be worth a lot of money, and cool cigarettes, which my friend Dicky Carstans started me with.

Grandpa, and I think my father, would help in advising us and supplying some of the building material, most of which was scrap wood and leftover material from new housing going up around the neighborhood.

In the Estonian culture, bonfires, as they were called, were a big part of festivals, picnics, and gatherings, so we were used to setting things on fire. Anyway, Bob Brockway, David, the Carroll boys, and I, as part of our junior fire department training would start and put out fires. And the one coming up was the last of the era.

The Hut was the victim of our last fire. We started a fire up in the loft, and when we thought it was too big an effort to put out, we went down to where the garden hose was connected to the faucet in the back lot. Little did we realize that my grandfather had shut the water off from the house for the winter. *No water.* Holy mackerel! Panic set in. What should we do?

The fire was burning down our hut, and we had no water. I remembered that we had one of those copper fire extinguishers that used baking soda, water, and acid. You turned it upside down, and the water would come out the little hose. I ran down to the house and barely was able to drag that thing up to the back woods to put out the burning hut, but it only made a dent in the fire. Then I told my brother to call the real fire department, which he did, and tell them just to send one truck, but of course, the whole department showed up. What a scene. Boy! Were we ever in trouble, big trouble.

Well, they were able to put out the fire in a few minutes, but the real damage came when my mother found out while working at the school cafeteria as a cook. The head custodian, George Wolf, who was working there also and who was in the real fire department, told my mother that there was a fire call in at 9 Roslyn Drive. She had to leave work, thinking that the big house was on fire. Boy, did I get it. To make matters worse, Bob Brockway's mother found out somehow that fire trucks were in her driveway, which bordered the back woods, and thought her house was on fire as well.

I had to go apologize to Mrs. Brockway, crying, and to put this whole era to an end, my mother ordered David and me to tear down the rest of the hut. That was the end of my firefighting career until I joined the real fire department when I turned eighteen years old. I stayed seven years as a volunteer with lots of early experience.

John, Byron And David Burning Leaves

Chapter 22

Seasons

Life growing up here in Glen Head in the late 1940s and early '50s was one big event after another. Between events, we had seasons, meaning some new interest we kids would dream up to have fun and to be creative. You must remember that we were surrounded by my father's talent in art, with paintings hanging up all over the house and in his studio and my grandfather's creative genius as a steam engineer and boat builder. We also grew up surrounded by lots of good music—the piano we all took lessons on, my father's hi-fi setup, and his accordion. Within this environment, we would invent these seasons, mostly based on what classic comic books were available, what we heard on the radio, and later on in our childhood, what was big on TV. That was a twelve-inch RCA black-and-white screen. I must say, though, my father but mostly Gramps would encourage us to dream. As an example, we built a fort like in the classic Robin Hood comics and played with homemade stick swords and shields made out of fruit basket lids. The fort was made out of cardboard boxes. Kids would come in and form teams. One side would defend the fort, and the other side would attack the fort. The big difference was that we built our own fort; there were no plastic playhouses that our parents bought in a toy store like Toys R Us. We made our own toys as well, sometimes with my grandfather's help, such as the hand-carved sword he made for me.

The big maple tree in the back woods, as we called it, was the site of the next big event, or in this case, the next big project. We kids would never sit still; we were always on the run, either thinking of something to build or how we could get into trouble. Most of the time, it was out of just plain stupidity or some innocent mistake.

My brother John, the oldest of the four kids, started this tree house in a maple tree, along with his friend George Hageman. The first floor was built some ten feet above the ground, and you had to use a ladder to get to it. This was a big deal to me at the old age of eight years old. This was like building a skyscraper in New York City to an eight-year-old; it was bigger than life. As I got a little older, I became my brother's helper and helped build the second story, which was like going to the moon. This tree house was the forerunner to the clubhouse, or "the Hut," as we called it, which caught on fire, as mentioned in the last chapter "The Junior Fire Department." Then things got really wild; this is the unheard "third story." It was the talk of the town, a three-story tree house. It had never been done in all of Glen Head history, as we kids thought. Challenges like this, to us, were just like following the footsteps of my grandfather, building a thirty-three-foot boat at the age of seventy. It runs in the family. No moss growing under anyone's feet here! I must say, the kids in our neighborhood were very creative. This creativity lingers on even today, like with me writing this book and being an artist at seventy. I guess it's a magical age. Tommy Malloy is creating metal sculptures and still lives across the street. He was part of the old gang more than a half century later.

This third story of the penthouse, a term we did not use then, was without my brother John, who by this time was in high school and had outgrown his interest in tree houses. He was more interested in girls and studying. He was a smart kid and eventually went on to Tuft's Medical School and became a pathologist. We were all proud of him. Anyway, this three-story tree house was a big deal to those kids who were "in the know" in Glen Head, and it lasted a long time. It was really a modern marvel of the time. Eventually, it was torn down, per the request of our parents, and was replaced by the Hut, which was another feat in itself.

The Skyscraper in the back woods

One of the seasons we kids enjoyed was the "bow-and-arrow" season, which was right out of this new invention called TV. You name it—the Lone Ranger and Tonto, Hop alon Cassidy, Gene Audrey and Trigger, and the list goes on. Well, the portrait my father painted of me says it all—it's me in a cowboy outfit holding a real gun. I remember it was heavy, unlike the plastic toy ones we would play with. It was something else just to hold that real gun.

What I am about to write about is pretty remarkable. My sister, Natalie, a few years ago, moved from Lancaster, Pennsylvania, to Delaware with her husband, and in the process, she had to downsize a lot of stuff. She gave me a box of toys we all grew up with, and Kay and I put it away in storage until recently when we started to unpack the box. Among the toys was a plastic bag with a plaid material in it. Well, it turned out to be the same shirt I wore as part of the cowboy outfit in the painting my father made of me. Almost seventy years later, the shirt is still intact and now on display in a shadowbox next to the painting of me holding that real heavy gun. Amazing.

1951

2017

Two incidents stand out in my mind. One of them was when some roofing guys were putting tar on a new roof on the garage, which was on the property behind my grandfather's back lot and the Springsteens' back lot as well. Now, since it was bow-and-arrow season, we kids shot these arrows made out of soft branches of the Lantos about 30 inches long onto the roof of the garage, driving those guys crazy. They were screaming and yelling at us kids to stop because the arrows were getting on the hot tar of the roof. One of the guys came off the roofing and down the ladder and started chasing us, but we, as natives of the territory, just melted into the woods, never to be found again.

The second incident occurred when I was not satisfied with just plain Lantos-branch arrows. Oh no! I had to have flaming arrows, like on TV. I took one of the oil rags my grandfather used in the garage to work on engines, soaked it with gasoline, and wrapped it around one of the arrows. I pulled back the string of the bow, and ... you guessed it. The arrow went forward, and the gasoline-soaked rag went in reverse. I got burned pretty badly all over my chest. Of course, I was not wearing a shirt, for how could you see the war paint on my chest when I was wearing a shirt? It would never happen!

The next big season was when we got a little older, around 1955 through 1957. I was around thirteen years old. It was rockets. Holy mackerel! Rockets were big then. With the launch and deployment of *Sputnik*, the first ever satellite to be put in orbit around the earth, by the Russians and the upcoming US attempt to do the same with the Vanguard rocket that blew up on the launch pad, it was time for us kids to make our mark in space.

I would clip and save all the photos and articles from the newspapers and study how these rockets worked. Now the boys, the ones who had the mental capacity to understand this new science, got together and decided to start our own program and join the race for space.

Since my father worked in the city, he went down to Chinatown in Lower Manhattan and bought the space engineers in Glen Head supplies. He mainly brought the basic ingredients for gunpowder: potassium nitrate, powder charcoal, and sulfur. We became, after trial and error, pretty good in making the gunpowder, which we used to fuel these babies—rockets, that is.

Rocket Headquarters—the Basement

This section gets a little rocket techie; you can skip it if you want.

So we would wrap *Life* magazine covers, which were cut into different-length strips—four, five, maybe six inches—roll them around a pencil or a dowel, and secure them with masking tape. My father would use a lot of masking tape for his artwork, and we had to use material that was readily available. The rocket engines were made with that same masking tape but wrapped around a six or eight penny nail (smaller than a pencil). Next, we would fit that rocket engine tightly into one end of these magazine-cover tubes, secure it with some straight pins, fill the rocket with the homemade gunpowder, and tape a stabilizer stick to the rocket body. Last, we would stick a piece of Jet-X readymade fuses into the rocket engine, and off to the launch pad we would go. The launch pad was a piece of cardboard left over from the forts of Robin Hood season. We folded it into a V, laid the rocket in the V, and lit the Jet-X fuse—and liftoff!

Trial and error and persistence paid off, and we were pretty successful in launching these little homemade rockets, with one going maybe a quarter mile high. Just as a side note, there are many rocket clubs today, mostly out West, from which you can buy factory-made rocket bodies, engines, and launch pads, with all the equipment, but we kids were the first rocket engineers and pioneered this field. We had a great growing-up experience with many fond memories.

But there was always room for some incident, and here was no exception. I was testing one of the secret formulas using aluminum power to make flares that would shoot out of the rocket top end when it reached a certain altitude like fireworks. Anyway, I poured some of this mixture on the street and threw a match on it to light it for a test. The match missed, so I flicked it over with my finger, and *poof*! It went off like a flash, and my hand got burned pretty badly. At that time, my parents were on a weekend trip, I think on my grandfather's boat, so I was left in big trouble. I needed to go to the emergency room at the Glen Cove Hospital. But how would I get there?

Ready? Mrs. Carroll—the mother of the Carroll boys, Randy and

Stephen, who were members of the junior fire company. Mrs. Carroll never left her zip code in the Willys Jeep she drove, and forget about the hospital in Glen Cove. Well, this was an emergency, so she had no choice. She managed to make it to the hospital and back, and my hand was all bandaged up with second-degree burns. What an ordeal, mostly for Mrs. Carroll.

The second incident was when we were mixing a new batch of gunpowder in the laboratory in the basement of our house, and one of the Bartell boys, either Richard or George, somehow accidently set off this match and got burned. There was smoke all over the basement and going upstairs into the house. Well, my mother then finally put the kibosh on the whole operation, and we had to shut down the Glen Head Space Program and leave all future operations to NASA.

Chapter 23

Tragedy at Sea

As I thought about writing this book and all of the stories that encompass the life of my grandfather, this chapter I really did not want to write. But in order to have the reader get the full scope of his life, I begin.

Can you picture a teletype coming across the telegraph machine, which some may remember from the TV series about World War II *Victory at Sea*, and the narrator speaking with a monotonic voice? For this event, it would sound something like this: "It was June 27, 1953. It was a sunny day, no wind, and the *Trijon* was about to shove off for another trip to the Long Island Sound, when a message came across the wire to 9 Roslyn Drive, Glen Head. It was seven thirty in the morning."

In this case, it was the phone. I answered the phone. It was Grandpa. "Byron, tell your father to get down to the boatyard right away; the boat is on fire."

As an eleven-year-old, it was beyond what I had experienced in life so far. I remember all I could do was yell out, "Dad! Dad! Grandpa's on the phone! Come here! Hurry, hurry up!"

Trijon on fire

No cell phones, no phone in every room, one line, one telephone, period! I think Ma and Dad were still in bed, as my father would a lot of times stay up late painting and Saturday morning was the only day he and Ma could sleep a little later. My father answered the phone, my mother got a little panicky, and the next thing I knew, they were gone, with camera in hand. I think my older brother, John, went with my father to the boatyard, and you can see from the photos, this was a tragic event.

You cannot begin to imagine the shock that went through this household, especially Gramps. All those memories—the great times, the fishing trips, the dry dock parties, all of the people who went on that boat, all through the weekends for years—the work and hardship, the sacrifice that went into building that boat some thirteen years earlier, gone, all gone, in minutes. Up in smoke! Boy!

There are several theories as to what happened, one of which was the gas line somehow got cut or damaged. The other was the gas tank. Gramps would never fill up the gas tank because he did not want too much gasoline on board, but this time, he was taking some friends out fishing, and they insisted on filling up the tank. Little did anyone know that apparently, there were some small holes at the top of the tank, and when they filled it up, the gasoline came up and overflowed through the holes into the bledge. When Gramps started up the engine, the whole boat pretty much exploded.

I understand that no one was hurt, except Gramps, who had his arms and face burned, and whether he went to the hospital, I don't know, but emotionally, it was not too good.

That day is one of those days you don't forget, even as a child of eleven. I don't remember too many of the details, but I do remember my brother John and I had the task of stripping the boat of all its hardware—the chrome moldings, clites, hooks, rope guides, hinges, and so on.

Amazingly, within a few hours that Saturday morning, from the time the fire started to when my father, brother, and I got to where the boat ended up, which was across the creek from the dock, thieves had already stolen the toilet and some hardware. It gave us all such a feeling of anger and sadness at how human beings can be so heartless in the time of tragedy and compound the feeling of sadness.

As you see from the photos my father captured with his Rolliflex camera, with which he had much experience, the *Trijon* was pushed out, off the dock, into the middle of the creek to prevent other boats from catching fire, as well as the dock itself. But that maneuver prevented the firemen, when they arrived, from putting water on the fire, which to this end totally destroyed Gramps's *Queen Mary*.

What a heartbreaking event. The whole neighborhood was in shock. Everyone came over to see Gramps, with his arms all bandaged up, to give their condolences and to express their grief with him. In the next few days, I don't remember exactly when, Gramps arranged for the carcass of the *Trijon* to come home to 9 Roslyn Drive.

John and Byron removing hardware

Chapter 24

Rebuild? Are You Crazy?

Nope!
You who are reading this book can now begin to realize why I am writing about this amazing man—Gramps. You got it! Rebuild! Yup! Gramps decided not to give up, not to quit, not to feel sorry for himself. No, not Gramps! "Let's move forward," he said. So the process began. Where do we start? How do we start? Well, I can remember some of the discussions between Gramps, my father and mother, Uncle Walter, and some of Gramps's friends, especially this guy Louie Slanenia. Louie was a cabinetmaker who lived down the street in the park where we lived. Louis was a key guy in the decision-making process because he would be responsible for building all the superstructure, meaning the insides, of the boat. Things like the interior parts of the yacht, the windows and trim, the control panel in the cabin, the seats, the bunk beds, the moldings, and all the rest of the cabin, which all had to be crafted out of mahogany lumber, the wood to use at this time in the boatbuilding era.

Grandpa and Louie rebuilding boat

Grandpa and Louie rebuilding boat

Hold it. But wait a minute! This was 1953, and this whole idea was insane. Why? Because Gramps was born in 1883 and that would make him seventy years old at that time. Think about it. Who in their right mind would build a boat of this size at the age of seventy? The only guy I know is Gramps. But not only would he rebuild the *Trijon* at this age; he decided to lengthen it another four feet to a total length of thirty-three feet. Come on! This was no rowboat. This was almost an oceangoing ship. I don't think the *Kantii* was this long.

Now, if you look carefully at some of the photos, you'll see clues as to what I am writing about. There was new lumber—and you don't use new lumber if you are going to just dismantle the remains of the *Trijon*. You are going to rebuild, and that's exactly what happened. So the story begins with how this seventy-year-old man pulled off this feat and how we kids got involved.

Gramps would engineer this adventure over a five-year period. He started with following the same lines as the original *Trijon* and joined a full-length piece of oak to the existing keel. From there, he bent the ribs, by first steaming them in a pipe with water at one end and a fire underneath. He then lifted the pipe on one end so the water would turn to steam and rise to the higher end of the pipe. The steam would make the wood soft, allowing it to be bent into shape, thus creating the structure of the boat, the ribs.

As you can see from the photos, it was a big engineering project, but Gramps pulled it off. We kids learned so much about building boats, steaming wood, having patience, and being precise. Some upbringing we had as kids. It gave us an edge to help overcome those challenges that we would face down the road. There is a saying, "Persistence is the key to victory."

Now we have to look at the big picture here. Gramps was seventy years old. Come to think about it, as I am writing this book, I'm seventy myself, and we (Gramps and I) at that age were still working full-time, Gramps at the National Casket Company in Long Island City and me at Dunkin' Donuts. Well, anyway, just a side note. I guess it runs in the blood, that Old World inheritance. Now working full-time in the city—that's what we called it then, anything west of Long Island was "the city"—how do you find time to build a thirty-three-foot boat? Two things: find the right person to help rebuild this boat and focus.

The first part is an interesting story and did not come to light completely until just a few years ago in November 2011 when I met Louis Slanenia's wife, Mary, who was eighty-eight years old at that time and was in excellent mental condition. Now Louie, whom I just mentioned, was the guy Gramps hired to help him rebuild this boat. Louie and Mary lived down in the park, as we called it, and Mary still lives there in the same house as I write this book. Now their next-door neighbors were the Bocks. The Bocks were an Estonian family; there were more than a few Estonian families in Glen Head. Mr. Bock worked with Gramps at the casket company. It's pretty interesting to me how people of the same ethnic background congregate together. Well, Mary said during their lunch break years ago, George Bock and Gramps were discussing this new adventure, and he mentioned his neighbor Louie was a cabinetmaker and was looking for work. Well, Louie got the job, and the rest is history. But it took over sixty years to tell this story. Interesting.

Gramps had a constitution that was incredible. He had the ability to focus and to keep his mind on whatever he did in life; this boatbuilding project was no exception. I remember Gramps coming home every evening in his new 1953 Henry J, and after eating dinner, he would immediately go to the back (yard) and start work. No getting sidetracked with stuff. No parties, drinking, or watching TV, except for the nightly news with Walter Windchill.

Laying out the keel, as seen in the adjoining photo, was the first big step in starting this undertaking. Next would be to cut the length of two-by-two-by-ten-inch or so oak ribs. Once steamed in the pipe setup, they were immediately taken to the keel and attached. They were bent to form to the template at the top of the would-be side of the boat, and this process was repeated over forty times to form the hull. This was some undertaking and took months to complete for just this part. Are you ready for this? Gramps put this hull together with *no blueprints*, just pure mental engineering. Amazing.

Grandfather

The form was an engineering feat in itself, maybe more like wood sculpturing or a 3-D art painting. The shape not only had to fit the line of the old boat, but it had to be a pattern that would not only encompass the new length of thirty-three feet from twenty-nine but be seaworthy as well. It had to be pleasing to the eye with long, sloping lines. My grandfather had to be able to see his boat in his head in its entirety, like an artist has to see the painting before his or her first brushstroke. My father (his son) had the same foresight, seeing things before they existed.

Once the ribs were in place and all attached, connecting both sides and meeting properly to the bow and the stern, then the form was removed. The planking would be the next step. It was a huge process.

This next part would be very much like the steaming of the ribs (not barbecue) but twice as difficult. Not only did the planks, which were white clear pine with no knots, have to be steamed and bent, but they had to be bent with a twist to conform to the shape of the hull. A compound bend and twist, sounds like a new disco dance, the bend and twist.

Okay, so we have the ribs in place and all of them connected to the keel. Now, the runners get screwed on to the ribs on the inside of the hull. (We'll call them "runners" for lack of another term.) The runners go from stem to stern or from the front of the structure to the rear. The runners hold the ribs in place, all of them evenly apart from one another. Now this whole structure looks like an upside-down fish but without the skin. The keel would be like the backbone of the fish but inverted. It is the bottom of the soon-to-be boat. Amazing how God designed fish to navigate through the water so naturally and easily and how humans, with God-given ingenuity, turned that fish design to the upside-down configuration of a fish to be used as a boat.

So now, the next step was the planking or the outside of the boat. Wood boats of this type and of this era used clear white pine with no knots, as mentioned previously. The planks would be cut to the correct length, and after they were steamed, which makes them pliable, they would be placed against the ribs and screwed into place using brass screws. This whole process started at the bottom, at the keel, and worked its way up, alternating the ends of the planks until they reached the top of the hull. Each brass screw before being used had to go into a countersink hole to be drilled through the cedar plank and into each rib. The countersunk hole had to be a certain depth so as to leave enough wood material to hold the two pieces of wood firmly together.

As two young kids then, we wanted to be part of this boatbuilding project, so Gramps assigned David and me to make plugs. What are plugs anyway? Well, all the planks that got screwed into place against those ribs, where all of those countersunk holes for those brass screws went in, had to be covered with those plugs of course. Plugs are little round cylinders the size of the screw holes. We had a special drill bit cutter attached to Grandpa's drill press, and by pressing down on a piece of pine, the same material as the planks, we would cut out those little pine cylinders that would fit into the screw holes. The plugs would be glued, chiseled off flush, and then eventually sanded and painted over. It was a real arduous process.

So now, we had a boat-looking structure that needed a top. That meant we were going to build a cabin on top of those ribs (not the ones you eat) and planks we just finished—thus the term, *cabin cruiser*. Wow, we were making progress. Remember, this whole process of building the cabin cruiser took five years to complete, by a man of seventy years old at the onset of this project.

But before the cabin started to take shape, the deck was next. The deck was the top of the boat, and at the front was the stern. The deck covered about one-third of the boat, using the same planking system as the sides, except we used teakwood, which goes on like flooring screwed to the rafters. They were attached from one side of the boat to the other, from the aft to the starboard. Teak comes from South America usually and was used because it's an oily wood that is very resistant to the salt water. It's an added bonus that it looks rich and is a very fine-grained wood. We used the same drill, screw, and plug method.

Okay, next the cabin stage started. This was where Louie, the cabinetmaker, began his real work. Now Louie made built-in bank furniture, where every piece of wood was precision made, fitted, and finished. That's why Gramps hired him, because he was the best in his trade. So now the cabin sides got cut out, not only to fit into the cabin space, but for the window, the cowl, the instruments, the galley area, the bunk beds, the kitchen area, the toilet, and the like.

At the same time, Gramps was designing, measuring, and assembling the engine, but what engine? Here we go again—a steam engine. A brand-new custom cabin cruiser powered by a steam engine. Boy oh boy, what are we getting into now? With Gramps around, anything could happen. Anyway, this steam engine was the same steam engine Gramps built some thirty years earlier and used in his first handmade seventeen-foot boat that he took us around Long Island Sound in. It was now restored with new bolder and all the stuff that goes with it—pipes, valves, flywheel, fitting, and so on. Also, there was the cooler condenser, transmission, drive shaft, propeller, coal bins, engine compartment, and much more.

The final touches were the windows, windshield, hardware, frames, electric wiring, lights, chrome trimming, paint, the galley stove, the icebox, and a can of Maxwell House coffee.

Just an interesting note as to Grandpa's intuition, every boat has a waterline. And the waterline is a line drawn on the bottom side of the boat to show where the water is going to be when the boat is placed in the water. So how do you know where that waterline is going to be painted on the side of the hull while it's still outside the water? You have to calculate the weight of the boat and shape of the boat and then figure it out. Well, Gramps, with his super judgment, drew the line and painted it, and when the boat went into the water, the water went right up to the line, perfect. Just amazing.

The final countdown began. After a once-over and walk around the *Trijon* a couple of times, a call went in to the boatyard. The boat trailer showed up within a short while to Glen Head, and they picked her up. After five long years of hard work and a few beers, off it went on June 18, 1959.

Ller Steams Up His Rare Craft

Glen Head—John Nernoff, who is operating at full steam at the age of 76, yesterday climaxed five years work by shoveling coal into the engine of a homemade cabin cruiser and launching the boat into Glen Cove Creek. The event: put the second steam-driven pleasure boat into Long Island's waters.

Although Nernoff is a steam engineer by trade, it wasn't just nostalgia for the piercing shriek of the steam whistle that led him to construct the 33-foot cruiser in the back yard of his home at 9 Roslyn Rd. He had what was left of two earlier boats to work with—the charred remains of his 29-foot gasoline-powered cruiser that exploded and burned in 1955 and the boiler and steam engine from the first boat he built in 1915.

Nernoff, a native of Estonia, brought a lot of know-how to his latest do-it-yourself task. He's

been building boats since he was 9 years old.

In his spare time for the past five years, between commuting three days a week to work in Long Island City and overseeing a family of children and grandchildren, he put together the Triton. The cruiser is named for himself, a son who is a commercial artist, and a grandson who is a Tufts graduate in Massachusetts. The three men share the name John. Nernoff estimates that he spent $4,000 on the Triton, whose confined steam engine operates at a pressure of 450 pounds for each square inch. The Triton, which runs on bituminous coal for five cents a mile, will be capable of a 200-mile sea trip. "But I don't think I'll be taking any long trips," Nernoff said. "I'll probably use it for fishing in the bay."

What is believed to be the only other steam-driven boat in Long Island waters is the 26-foot Little Effie, run by Capt. Lauren McCready of Kings Point Merchant Marine Academy.

GATHERING STEAM. John Nernoff, 76, shovels coal into steam engine, above, as he takes his homemade 33-foot cruiser out for first run, left, in Glen Cove yesterday. Nernoff, a steam engineer, built both boat and engine in his back yard.

Newsday

Free, June 19, 1957

Chapter 25

The Tranny

In my adolescent days, I was always interested in building things. As we talked about in previous chapters, my environment was creative here in this house with my father's artwork and his baking. My father loved to bake pies and cakes. He baked the creamiest pumpkin pie you've ever had, and his apple pie was the best, with lots of spices. This love of baking is reflected in some of his paintings of his handiwork.

The same is true with my grandfather, who also had this drive, the desire to build, accomplish, and finish his projects. There were two boats, the house, the 1931 Pontiac, the wall, and many other projects he completed. All of these projects were finished and without him quitting.

Well, I picked up this same spirit, and it is still true today, as mentioned in earlier chapters. For one, I am writing this book, taking after my father in painting, and gardening, featuring the victory garden and the raspberry patch in the back lot. My father's and grandfather's attitude and this spirit still linger, even today.

Top left Photo Original 31 Pontiac
Middle Right: Finished hot rod

Well, let's get on with the story about the tranny. The first really big project I was involved with, besides the clubhouse in the back woods, which we set on fire, the soapbox wagons, model airplanes, gunpowder rockets, and the list goes on, was the coupe. This coupe, as it was called, was my grandfather's 1931 Pontiac five-window coupe. He originally put it together years before out of parts from other cars, but basically it was a 1931 Pontiac body on a 1928 Chevy frame with a four-cylinder Chevy engine. Well, after my older brother, John, used it in high school, like how I became head resident of the attic after he grew out of it, I inherited the '31 and used it myself for a short while. You know, it was that hand-me-down generation we all grew up with.

At this time, hot-rodding had started to become popular. And me, being someone who needed to be on the edge of something new, I had to get involved. Well, the '31 was still registered with my grandfather, but something had to be done. Needless to say, the old four-cylinder was an embarrassment to have sitting on the frame of the coupe so we had to do something. Everyone in the know was now into hot-rodding and tooling around in a street machine, and I was making believe with this four-banger, always with the hood closed. I started to ask around, to see what the best engine would be to replace this embarrassment. And it turned out to be a small-block eight-cylinder Chevy engine. Now in 1955, General Motors introduced a 265 CI eight-cylinder engine, which was such a success. Then two years later, they came out with 283 CI engine. Well, everyone wanted the 283 version, therefore making the 265 CI very available and affordable, so that was going to be the engine of choice and the replacement of the old four-cylinder engine.

Now we were getting serious, so ownership was important, and building a hot rod and having it owned by my grandfather was not going to happen. So Gramps, with the heart of gold that he had, sold the '31 to me for ... Are you ready? One dollar. You had to have some monetary value of a sale to register a vehicle anyway, but for a dollar, that's beautiful.

So, here we go. We picked up that 265 somewhere, and now thinking about it, I think we bought it from Trotter's junkyard in Sea Cliff, which turned out to be the home away from home for us

1950s hot-rodders. After many nights in the garage, spent figuring and measuring, Gramps, who helped when he got home from work, and I finally put together some engine mounts that would hold the engine to the frame. There were many other components that had to be designed, such as fuel lines, wiring, battery setup, and steering box, just to mention a few. Just the mere fact that this eight-cylinder engine had to fit where this tiny four cylinder was, was a feat to be reconciled.

The final step in this hot-rod conversion was the transmission, or the tranny as we called it; it needed to be attached to the engine and then to the drive shaft and then to the rear axle. What do we use? Not knowing the power and torque of this new contraption of an engine, Gramps figured we'd just use the old tranny that came with the four banger. So I looked around and bought this bell housing that was meant for a more substantial tranny. Gramps, with his steam-engineering experience, reworked this bell housing to fit the four cylinder engine tranny with the bolt pattern and shaft length measurements.

The big day, what a scene. You can't imagine, a fifteen- or sixteen-year-old kid and his grandpa, starting up this contraption, this huge engine sitting in the tiny frame. You couldn't even see the frame. Now we started up this engine with everyone in the neighborhood looking on. What a scene. The engine started, smoke coming out of the exhaust pipes, engine shaking, holy mackerel. This was really something to see.

Then, after a little adjustment to the carburetor and slight turn of the distributer, Gramps motioned to me—because we could not talk over the loud sound of the open pipes with no muffler—to get into the driver's seat and take it up Depot Place for a ride.

Okay, here we go. I put it in first gear, let out the clutch, and started up the street. Gramps yelled out, "Give it a little gas!" and so I did. Well, within a few seconds up the street, there was a huge explosion that was heard all over the neighborhood. The tranny was in million pieces all over the road with a trail of tranny fluid like a snake following the coupe. There we were, me not knowing anything about auto engineering at this point, and Gramps being a steam engineer. This new technology on the V8's was very awakening. So Gramps, the neighborhood boys, and I rolled the coupe back into the garage, and Gramps and I reworked the design. We did not give up, and the next section will tell how we made it to the West Hampton drag strip.

So the coupe was sitting in the garage with no transmission. Hmmm! Now what! Back to our home away from home, you guessed it—Trotter junkyard. The steering committee, get it? The steering committee, or maybe a better term would be the transmission committee, were looking for a replacement tranny, but what you have to realize is that in 1959, this is all new stuff for us kids, uncharted territory. There were no hot-rod shops around then. You had to go to a car dealer or junkyard and figure it out for yourself. After a few weeks of searching, asking for advice, getting opinions, and groping in the dark, we got a general consensus—a 1939 Buick transmission. It had a four-speed on the floor direct to the transmission. There were no automatics then, and it was designed for a heavy automobile with a big engine. At the time, a Buick straight 8 was a big engine. It was eight cylinders all in a row, putting out enough horsepower to drive that big Buick body and frame. The second reason a Buick transmission was selected was that it had a torque tube drive shaft set up that had to fit the '31's rear end, which could have been a 1934 Chevy rear since the front end of the coupe was a '34 Chevy knee action front end, but I'm not really sure. This knee action front had built-in shock absorbers, advanced technology at the time.

Interestingly enough and conveniently, the bell housing that Gramps had adapted to fit the original '28 Chevy tranny was originally designed for a Buick tranny to fit a small-block Chevy engine to begin with. So converting it back to fit a Buick tranny was relatively easy. Now we had to find a '39 Buick tranny. I am not positive, but I think my friend Bobby Izzo got this tranny for me. Now Bobby was the guy to know because he was into building hot rods himself. Bobby lived over in the Glen Cove area, not too far from Glen Head, and his father owned a sand and gravel business and had a huge excavation in the East Norwich / Oyster Bay area. Bobby had access to a complete and fully equipped garage, which was used to maintain the fleet of trucks for the family sand and gravel business.

After the tranny was bolted to the bell housing, with all the clutch mechanics lined up and adjusted, then fitted to the torque tube drive shaft and finally to the rear end, everything looked like it was going to work, so we rolled the coupe out of the garage and started it up just like before. Praise the Lord, this time, there was no explosion and everything seemed to work well.

So we had a full fender '31 Pontiac coupe with a '34 Chevy front end, 265 small-block Chevy engine with a two-barrel carbonator, and a '39 Buick tranny. We were off and running.

Just as a side note, since Grandpa was a steam engineer and was used to all the steam equipment and stuff, he used plumbing pipes for the exhaust and for the running boards. Guess what he used. Sewer grates. Yep, sewer grates, because the rain and snow would just run through the grates with no rust or corrosion then. Smart thinking.

I used the coupe as my main car for everyday use and of course drag racing. I went off with the coupe to college, which was the Culinary Institute of America in New Haven, Connecticut, to study culinary arts and hotel administration. It was on the Yale University campus. We had lot of fun with that coupe, and it ran well. Everything went fine until the big crash. Oh no, now what? I was going my normal speed (fast) coming from school to my apartment when some guy ran his stop sign. I jammed on my brakes, but I hit him broadside anyway. Well, needless to say, the coupe was pretty much irreparable, but I did not want it to be towed to some junkyard where all that work would be lost in a pile of scrap metal. So now what? Well, here we go again, I called my friend Bobby Izzo. He came up to New Haven with his car trailer, and we took it back home to Long Island.

After the coupe sat in the backyard for some time—I don't know how long, but I had finished college—I knew that I had to build a hot rod. I couldn't just let the '31 body sit there, but I didn't even know where to begin. Then one day, Tommy Malloy, one of those original boys who pushed the coupe back into the garage after the tranny explosion a few years back, came over to the house and said, "Hey, Byron! You know there's an old car frame with the tires still on it just sitting there doing nothing at the boatyard down in Glen Cove? It's down where Grandpa kept his first boat. I think someone used it as a boat trailer at one time, so let's go and take a look!" So my brother David and I went to check it out, and surprisingly, it looked like something that might work as a frame for this new hot rod.

I had already taken the old '31 Pontiac apart, dumped whatever was left of the wreck, and kept the body itself. That's the coupe body with the five windows. We needed some basic measurements to see if the body and frame would be a marriage, and it was. So we went down to the boatyard, using David's car, which had a tow hitch set up, and towed the frame back to Glen Head. Another side note, guys with boats in those days would use old car frames, bolt down wood planks, load their boats on top, and use it as a boat trailer. In addition, the area where this frame was, was also the city dump, so finding the frame there was not that unusual.

This time around, this was going to be a real hot rod. Hot-rodding was really big by then in the early 1960s. I was not about to be left out, and so the work began. The '31's body fit right over the '36 Ford pickup frame, as it turned out that it was, and it looked beautiful. Wow. It had that racked look, channeling as it was called. It really looked cool. Since my hot-rod buddy Bobby Izzo had all that experience in building hot rods, he said he would help me mount the body to the chassis. So we towed the chassis and the body over to the sand pits in East Norwich and into the truck garage. Within a week or so, we had figured out where the mounts would go, welded them to the '36 Ford chassis, and then bolted the '31 to the mounts. We then got it back to Glen Head and into Grandpa Nernoff's garage.

So next was the installation of the drive train. Train? Something for the reader to figure out. Bobby came through with a new 327 CI small-block Chevy engine, which we put together with a three-speed Chevy tranny. It had a Hurst side-mounted floor shifter connected to a '56 Chevy rear end, compliments of Trotter's junkyard. This time, there was no tongue tube setup. I bought my own set of torches and an arc welder and went to town. I designed my own rear suspension, engine mounts, tranny mounts, steering mounts, and so on. Now my old buddy from across the street, Tom Malloy, taught me how to weld and cut steel with the torches. We used a '40 Ford front end, and the list goes on.

When the rear suspension was designed and ready for welding, I used some of the boiler pipes that Gramps had left over from the boiler he had installed for the hot water heater in the house. I then built the traction bars that were welded to the rear end, and we went for a test run. Here we go again. For the third time, we rolled out the coupe from the Nernoff garage, started the engine, and took off up the street. Well, this time, the tranny worked perfectly, but the traction bars twisted around the rear end like two pretzels. I didn't realize that you can't use boiler pipe because it's made from soft steel. So back into the garage, a familiar trip, where I rebuilt the traction bars, this time out of angle iron. This solved the problem. We did another test run, and everything worked as planned.

After the hot rod was almost together, we made the final touches and just in time, because in two weeks, I would be drafted into the army. It was June 1964. We had a big caravan of guys who followed us out to the West Hampton racetrack, where I did a 109 miles per hour in the quarter of a mile without second gear and won a trophy—B Altered. There is a saying, "Persistence is the key to victory." The following week, I went off to Fort Dix, New Jersey, for basic training and spent two years serving my country as an army MP.

Chapter 26

The Hat

Grandpa original hat in front

I love to work in the garden. When we kids were growing up here in Glen Head in the late 1940s and '50s, my parents and grandfather were always either growing vegetables in the victory garden or building fishponds surrounded by lots of flowers and lots of rocks, North Shore rocks[1] that is, and lots of azalea bushes, over thirty in number at the time. (See photos.)

Well, we were all indoctrinated in growing things and were also taught to take care of the chickens. Yes, we had it all, even chickens. We spent a lot of time outside with all these activities, which meant exposure to the sun. As our Estonian heritage graced us with fair skin, blue eyes, and blond hair, we were always being told by my mother, "Don't forget to wear a hat!"

Baseball hats are very popular today as the hat of choice along with other types of hats. But in those earlier days, as you can see in some of the photographs in this book, fedora hats were very popular. Fedora hats were worn for many occasions, and I guess after being used for many years, being made out of wool-type materials, they would wear out and be used for other purposes, like working in the garden. That is exactly what my grandfather did with one of his fedora hats; he wore it while he worked in the garden, landscaped the multilevel yard with these North Shore rocks, and built his boat, which is one of the features in this book.

Well, his hat went through the war, shall we say, with a lot of life's experiences and much wisdom, and it also protected his head from the sun. Well, I still have and wear his hat, with all of the tears and holes and stains. It is special since so much of my grandfather's spirit goes along with the hat. Of course, the hat itself has no spiritual significance, only the Lord can give us that, but wearing the hat reminds me of those days of working hard, treating people with love and respect, and relying on God for a reason to live the good life, shall we say. That is how we should live today.

My grandfather was a guy everyone respected, and the whole neighborhood knew and called him Grandpa Nernoff, and, of course, to the people closer to him, he was "Gramps."

---

[1] North Shore rocks are rocks that are collected from the north shore of Long Island and locally surrounding areas, which we used to build the rock garden here in Glen Head. South Shore rocks come from the south shore of Long Island; they are smooth and a sandy beach color. North Shore rocks are mixtures of granite and gray marble-looking rock. A lot of them are left from the ice age.

Disappointments, tragedies, and victories that was his life. He never gave up, just kept going, as he would say, and his hat reminds us of that attitude that we should all keep and strive for. You don't live over a hundred years for nothing. You have to have that *something* in life and, of course, relying on and walking with the Lord gives that zest to life.

Chapter 27

Out of the Ashes

Interesting phrase, "out of the ashes." It is a saying usually associated with something good that comes out of something not so good or what's left over from out of a fire, like a treasured item.

Clay Lots

Ashes are mentioned a few times in this book. The first time was in the chapter when I talked about our grandfather coming out to Glen Head, Long Island. He came out from the city and bought a couple of residential building lots not too far from where he built this house, which is why this whole book got started and what it is based on. It turned out that the ground that the lots were on was all clay, not suitable to build on. After Gramps did a soil test, he exchanged the ground for two lots farther west up the hill where we live now. The two original lots were excavated over the years to make bricks. Post Bricks was the name of the company that supplied the bricks used to build many structures on Long Island, New York City, and other places.

When the land was totally excavated and there was no more clay left, it was no longer useful. Now what? They had to stop the whole operation, not just because they ran out of clay, but also because they hit underground streams and water. We kids used to play in the new pond and would catch frogs—big ones.

Now this big hole in the ground was then filled up with—guess what. Ashes. Wow, where did so much ash come from? It came from Long Island Lighting Company's power plant, located down the street in Glenwood Landing at the waterfront, where coal was burned to heat the water and create stream, which turned the turbines to generate the electricity that powered half of Long Island at that time. The ash was buried for years in that big hole in the ground until it was full and then was capped off with top soil. Years later, developers were planning to build houses on the property and discovered that the ground was unsuitable to hold any kind of structure because of the ash. It wasn't suitable for much except for ... ready? A baseball field. This field is still in use today. The kids love it, and "out of the ashes" came a blessing. The pond is still there too, although it's now fenced in so no more frog hunting.

Ashes were next mentioned when Grandpa's first boat burned up. (See the chapter "Tragedy at Sea.") That was a sad time in our family history, especially in his life, and those ashes from Gramps's boat were left on the bottom of Glen Cove Creek. But in Grandpa's life, many of those ashes were turned into victories, and he ended up after more than 101 years on earth with the ultimate victory, his place in heaven, sailing with Jesus on the Sea of Galilee.

So how we are getting any closer to the real story about ashes? Back in the old days, as they say, coal was the main source of heat, and of course, that went for us here in Glen Head as well. Many families here had coal-burning furnaces, including the Malloys, who lived across the street. Now the coal-burning furnace that heated our house was built by the big steam engineer of the house, Grandpa Nernoff. He really was a steam engineer. Ours was the best furnace in town. It came complete with all of the amenities—coal bin, special coal shovel, pokers, ash racks, ash pails, and ash cans.

The coal bin was a space in the basement next to one of the basement windows. When the coal-delivery guy came, he would extend the shoots that were connected to the truck, which was full of coal. The coal traveled down through the open window and would pile up in the coal bin inside the basement. The bin had to be close to the furnace so it would be convenient to shovel.

We kids couldn't wait for the coal guy to come. We loved to watch the coal come down the shoot and pile up in the coal bin, and then we would play in it. Our mother would yell at us kids to get out of that coal bin because we would track coal dirt all over the house.

The coal shovel had a deep scoop in its design to allow for a lot of coal, and it helped to prevent spillage. Pokers and ash racks were made out of six- to seven-foot three-quarter-inch steel rods with oval-shaped handles so they were easy to grip. The poker was used to break up the burned coal, or what we called clinkers, and then when the fire cooled off a little, the ash would fall through the racks and collect on the bottom of the furnace, which would then be scraped up as ash and shoved into the ash pail.

We children had to learn this system because when Gramps was at work or out on his boat for an extended period of time, somebody had to keep the heat and hot water going. My mother was the number-one furnace master; she knew how to make the best stoked coal fire. Gramps would bank the furnace before going to work at five in the morning and it would last until three or four in the afternoon when he would get home just to do it all over again for the night so that everyone would be warm and comfortable. I remember being told we couldn't burn a lot of newspaper because it would build up too much carbon, which means it wouldn't burn clean and would stick to the water pipes in the furnace, reducing the heat conductivity.

So now the ash was not thrown out in the garage, we used to take it up to the garden in the back lot and use it for fertilizer, which is where term *potash* comes from. It was also used for driveways because it became sort of solid when wet and would pack down, excellent to drive on. Gramps also sprinkled the ash on all of the walks, so we would not slip on the ice.

Just a side note, I remember my older brother, John, and I burned up my mother's extra sewing machine strap. She used it on us when we were bad once too often, so it went into the fire in the furnace and became part of the ash, never to be found again.

Okay, so let's get down to the real reason for this chapter about ash. Linda Carroll now lives in the Boston area but back then lived up the street here in Glen Head. Linda is Randy and Steven Carroll's sister, and she called the other day. We were discussing this book, and she brought up the fact that Grandpa Nernoff would be very protective of all the neighborhood kids. And in the winter, we would sleigh ride down Depot Place, the side street we all would play and congregate on, ending up on Roslyn Drive, which had a lot of traffic. Grandpa would shovel the ash at the bottom of Depot Place, preventing the sleigh from going any further, which kept us from going onto Roslyn Drive. Because of his ingenious use of ash, we are all still alive today.

So now, recycling is a big business today, with bottles, cans, newspapers, and even outdated computers and electronics, but the pioneer of this industry was Grandpa Nernoff, who was in the forefront of many things, including *ash*.

Chapter 28

Aunt Rose's Bread

This was a letter Kay and I sent out to all of our friends and neighbors one Christmas, along with this bread and with Kay's homemade chocolate-chip cookies. I baked Aunt Rose's bread, as we named it here in the Glen Head house. So here it is.

Merry Christmas
2008

The brief history behind this bread along with some eating instructions:

When I was a small boy in the 1940s and 1950s, my parents used to take me and my two brothers and sister to see my aunt Rose in Gordon, Connecticut, several times a year. You see, my father's mother passed away when she was in her forties, so my aunt Rose (her sister) became like his surrogate mother, and we kids became her grandchildren or something like that. Anyway, my Aunt Rose was a very good cook, and she would always make good stuff when we came to visit: lobster dinners (twenty-five cents a pound then), cucumber and sour cream salad, raspberry jelly, and German pancakes (like crepes) rolled up with this raspberry jelly she made from her raspberry patch in the backyard, among many other favorites—and, of course, Aunt Rose's famous homemade bread.

Years later, after Aunt Rose passed away, my father picked up the bread-making responsibility and started making this bread, Aunt Rose's bread, as we all called it, and now I am keeping the tradition going. I hope you will enjoy this bread with a little bit of its history.

In order to savor this once-in-a-lifetime experience, you can eat the bread two ways: One way is to eat it plain and untoasted with real butter, and the slices should be 5/8 to 3/4 inch in width. If you use anything other than real butter and I find out about it, you will be cut off from any future bread gifts. The other way (preferred) is to toast the bread at the recommended width, butter it, and use the raspberry jelly enclosed. It's not Aunt Rose's jelly, but close. Again, if I find out you used some other kind of jelly like grape or marmalade, you're cut off.

Enjoy!
God bless you,
Byron and Kay

PS. Kay enclosed her famous homemade chocolate-chip cookies, and by far, they're the best you have ever had—bar none.

Chapter 29

Job

Who is Job? Does my grandfather know him? I hope so! Job's life was very much like my grandfather's, a life of disappointments, tragedy, and failures. But in the end, because of their courage, faith, endurance, and walk with the Lord, both Job and Gramps ended up as heroes to God and to us and left a life of amazement and admiration.

By this time, you all know much about Gramps, but who is this guy Job? Maybe some Estonian friend of his? Nope. Job is a man in the Old Testament whom God chose to be tested by the devil and to show the world how he overcame many of life's obstacles and difficulties. In the end, he made it into the Bible as one of God's heroes. I see Gramps also as one of God's heroes who made it into this book. We can learn the business of living through these two godly men.

Chapter 30

The End

We have come to the end of this book. We have read about a man who was full of life, was an accomplisher, and worked hard in everything he did. Our grandpa, John Nernoff Sr., was not only our friend but our hero, a man we could trust. Gramps, in the end of his life here on earth, said to me in the nursing home in Roslyn, Long Island, New York, "I am tired of living"—and who wouldn't be at 101 1/2 years old?

My wife and I went to a funeral a few years ago of a longtime Christian lady and friend, Joy Levi, who went home to be with her Savior. She was just like our grandfather; she had the same character traits, worked hard, had a big heart, and was a doer and lover of life. This is what was printed on her funeral card:

Grandpa Nernoff 1983 (100 years old)

THE WHITE HOUSE

WASHINGTON

June 30, 1982

Dear Mr. Nernoff:

Congratulations on your 100th birthday!

Nancy and I are delighted to send our warmest wishes
on your special day and our hopes for continued joys
and blessings.

Sincerely,

Ronald Reagan

Mr. John Nernoff, Sr.
c/o Mr. Jon Nernoff, Jr.
9 Roslyn Drive
Glen Head, New York 11545

I'm Free
I'm following the path God laid for me
Don't grieve for me, for now I'm free
I took his hand when I heard him call
I turned my back and left it all

I could not stay another day
To laugh, to love, to work or play
Tasks left undone must stay that way
I found that place at the close of day

If my parting has left a void
Then fill it with remembering joy
A friendship shared, a laugh, a kiss,
Ah yes, these things I too will miss.
Be not burdened with time of sorrow
I wish you the sunshine of tomorrow
My life's been full, I've savored much
Good friends. Good times, a loved one's touch

Perhaps my time seemed all too brief
Don't lengthen it now with undue grief
Lift up your heart and share with me
God wanted me now, He set me free.

My grandfather was not much of a religious man, as far as I could see, but I have his Estonian Bible, and in those days, if you had one or two books, that was your library. To have one of those books be the Bible, well, maybe that is saying something. All I know is that Gramps had all the makings of a man right out of the Bible. He had courage to take on challenges in life, which doesn't come out of thin air; it has to come from a higher source. He had faith to trust God for some sense of wisdom and morals, which Gramps portrayed in his daily life, as those who grew up with him witnessed. Gramps would never say anything bad about a person. Last but not least, he had ethics, particularly a work ethic. Gramps would never stop. His favorite saying was "Just keep going," and he would wave his hand forward at the same time. Just keep going.

The End

About the Author

I was born in 1942 here on Long Island of Estonian Parents and grew up in Glen Head along with my two brothers and a sister and my Grandfather. My father was an artist and my grandfather was a licensed steam engineer. We had a treasured upbringing, being surrounded by many of my father's paintings and my grandfather boat building skills. Our Estonian heritage with my grandparents being emigrants from that country and living in the house built by my grandfather in 1919, it seems a wanting challenge to write a book about this unique and blessed family. My mother saved every photograph (many thousands) my Father took and every family document along with photos dating back to the 1800's. Many people have encouraged me to put all of this history in to writing or otherwise it would all be lost.

So here it is "Memories from the Attic"